The Grieving
Parent's
Book of Hope

The Grieving Parent's Book of Hope

How to Survive the Loss of Your Child

NORMA SAWYERS-KURZ

DOGWOOD PUBLISHING
BOLIVAR, MO 65613
WWW.DOGWOODPUBLISHINGUSA.COM

Published by Dogwood Publishing, Bolivar, MO

"Scripture taken from the NEW AMERICAN STANDARD BIBLE®, Copyright © 1960, 1962, 1963, 1968, 1971, 1972, 1973, 1975, 1977, 1995 by The Lockman Foundation. Used by permission." www.Lockman.org

Printed in the United States of America

Publisher's Cataloging-in-Publication
(Provided by Quality Books, Inc.)

Sawyers-Kurz, Norma, 1943-
    The grieving parent's book of hope : how to survive the loss of your child / Norma Sawyers-Kurz.
    pages cm
    Includes bibliographical references and index.
    LCCN 2013947140
    ISBN 9780963003188 (softcover)
    ISBN 9780963003164 (hardcover)
    ISBN 9780963003171 (e-book)

    1. Grief. 2. Children--Death. 3. Parents--Psychology. 4. Adjustment (Psychology)   I. Title.

BF575.G7S299 2014   155.9'37'085
                          QBI13-600141

Dedication

To Neal, Hunter, and Landon,
my three grandsons, who have been
a great blessing in my life

Contents

Blessed are those
who mourn, for they
shall be comforted.

— Matthew 5:4

Introduction

You have lost your child. In your heart you have come to know deepest pain. Your grief has brought emotional suffering that seems beyond your own capacity to survive. Your soul cries out with a sense of despair that feels so overwhelming. You feel incredibly powerless, deeply helpless, and seemingly hopeless.

It may be difficult for you to believe right now, but you can survive this tragedy. I know you can, because I have survived myself what you have experienced: the loss of a child. Here is the personal story of my own struggles after the death of my child.

A Hint of Sorrow

It was Christmas 1981. A festive mood filled the atmosphere of our modest farm house as my loved ones and I gathered about our glittering Christmas tree surrounded by gaily wrapped presents. My eyes moved to my good-looking son and daughter, sixteen and fifteen, as they happily opened their gifts. I was so proud of them with their strong, young bodies and intelligent minds.

Suddenly, as I watched my children tearing paper from their packages, the air around me became kaleidoscopic with memories dancing merrily about like the tinsel reflections on our glittering tree. My thoughts retreated sixteen years to a Christmas long ago and to a baby boy, soft as silk, snuggled against my breast, his small body bathed in the warm light of our twinkling tree. Time moved onward another year to the gurgle of laughter as the baby boy, now a toddler, "hid" from me behind a similar Christmas tree while I rocked his newborn baby sister to sleep, her tiny head reposing peacefully upon my shoulder. Year by year, the remembrances passed in memory's eye. Two little tots with stars in their eyes opened presents on early Christmas morns. Squeals of delight were heard as velvety stuffed animals and brightly-colored pull toys were clutched to their small chests. As the years flashed by, a parade of dolls, trains, trucks, and games marched before my recollection until suddenly the small tykes had changed to splendid teenagers.

Abruptly returning to the present, I felt a familiar surge of gratefulness for my wonderful family. In bygone days I had often felt a wonder that I had been blessed with my beautiful children. Now, once again, my gaze fell upon my beloved son David, his fawn-colored hair shining in the luminous glow of the tree, and upon my daughter Karen, her light hair catching the nuance of colors from the flickering bulbs. I could hardly believe my good fortune.

We were carefree that Christmas Day in 1981, not realizing that soon our circumstances would change. The next week passed normally until one cold evening when we all sat gathered around our television. It was a tradition at our home to watch football during the holiday season, and this winter was no exception. Family members had been continually engrossed that week in watching the sport, but Karen and I were bored.

Turning to me, she sighed, "Mom, do you want to go into the bedroom and read to one another while they watch football?"

I replied, "That's an excellent idea."

From the time my son and daughter were small, they had always enjoyed having me read to them. Reading was the source of many of our best times. Over the years I had read story after story to my children, but now we had graduated to reading to each other.

Gathering up several issues of *Reader's Digest*, my daughter and I snuggled under the covers to read to one another. After reading several articles, we came to a story which touched our hearts deeply. We were both so overcome with emotion that we had to take turns reading.

At the time we had no way of knowing that the narrative we had just read would indirectly affect our lives forever. The written account was not only a hint of sorrow which would soon enter our lives, but also an instrument which God would later use in a remarkable way to change my entire life.

TRAGEDY

March 4, 1982, the day before my daughter's tragic accident, is etched in my mind forever. I have relived that day and those following it a thousand times.

Although usually an outgoing person, there were times when Karen could be introverted. Both aspects of her personality were evident the day before her accident. On that afternoon Karen was particularly quiet. She came in after school, pulled up a stool, and watched television while I finished my work. My daughter seemed to have something on her mind. Later that evening the outgoing aspect of her personality was evident as she and her brother wrestled around playing "horse" after supper.

Karen always had a good sense of humor. That night as I was doing dishes, I asked her to come dry them for me. She replied, "Oh, Mom, I can't. I've got a broken leg!" Then she hopped into the kitchen on one leg as if the other were broken.

After my family went to bed that Thursday night, I thumbed through a seed catalog forming plans for planting a garden later in the spring. Plans were also running through my mind concerning a spring house-cleaning project for the weekend. I had no idea that my happy plans would soon change.

Tragedy struck on Friday, March 5, 1982. Finishing with my last customer at my beauty salon, I glanced up at the clock to notice it was 3:05 p.m. The busy week was almost over, and my attitude was cheerful as I contemplated the weekend. As I was handing change to the customer, a young high school boy came running into the shop flinging his arms around aimlessly.

I wondered, *What is wrong with that boy?* He was so overcome with emotion he was speechless, but finally regained his composure sufficiently to tell me Karen had been involved in an accident. Immediately, my husband at the time (David and Karen's dad), and I started sprinting toward the scene of the accident one block away. As I ran, I reasoned that the boy's urgency was undue alarm. I told myself repeatedly that the accident was probably a minor mishap; surely it was nothing serious.

When we arrived at the scene, someone tried to restrain me, but I pulled away; I had to see about my daughter. Horrified, I saw her lying unconscious on the street, her eyes fixed and staring. People familiar with first aid were administering CPR and doing everything they could to keep her alive.

I don't believe it, I thought. *It's not true! Karen will be all right. My daughter and I are fighters. I will stay by her side until she recovers. She will be all right.* In a stupor from the shock of Karen's situation, I watched as she continued to receive first aid. *This is unreal*, I kept thinking. *Any moment now I will wake up and find this to be a bad dream.*

In hushed silence a large group of bystanders, friends and relatives, gathered all around us. Karen's brother was standing with his head leaned against a parked truck; our son had walked up on the scene of his sister's accident. My heart reached out to him. But I was numb, too numb to cry. Fear, frustration, disbelief, grief, shock — these emotions and others now belonged to our family, to our relatives, and to our friends.

But how had this calamitous accident happened? Earlier our daughter had decided to cut a school friend's hair. The two were riding the boy's motorcycle on their way from school when a feed truck hit them at an intersection. The force of the collision threw both riders toward a car waiting at a stop sign. Karen was thrown under the car, her helmet came off, and her head struck the pavement. Fortunately for the boy, his helmet remained intact as he was thrown from the motorcycle into the right rear tire of the car. He suffered a severe concussion and multiple fractures but later recovered completely.

As we waited for the ambulance to arrive, time seemed to stand still. Trembling with fear for Karen, I wondered, *What is taking them so long? Don't they know my daughter could be dying?* Finally, the wailing ambulance rushed up to the scene. After examining Karen's condition, the medical attendants decided to transport our daughter to a small, nearby hospital to stabilize her condition. Numb with panic, I accompanied my daughter on the trip. Again and again, I tried to convince myself that Karen was going to be alright. Yet I felt so frightened. My mouth became so dry that my tongue felt like cotton. I watched as the paramedic worked with my daughter in the ambulance. *Just keep at it,* I thought to myself. *Keep working with her. She'll come through.*

Although the ride to the hospital seemed to take forever, at last we sped into the hospital emergency entrance. Breathing heavily, I followed the attendants as they rushed Karen into the building. A feeling of intense fear swept over me as I watched my daughter disappear into the emergency room. Suddenly, I felt that I had to sit down. After a period of time, a doctor came to inform us that Karen's condition was critical. Feeling certain the physicians at a larger hospital would have a better prognosis, I told myself this doctor was mistaken.

After waiting for some time, we were taken to the hospital chapel. I thought we had been taken there to pray for Karen, but others were afraid we were in the chapel to learn she had died. A nurse started to tell us something about our daughter but was interrupted by a doctor who informed us that Karen was to be transferred to larger hospital facilities. Watching as they reloaded our daughter for the trip, we were told by the ambulance attendants that I couldn't ride with Karen this time. We followed the ambulance in our car until mechanical problems forced us to finish our trip with relatives. Everything was going wrong.

The ride seemed endless. Karen was in the ambulance, and we had no idea what was happening. We didn't even know if she was still alive. My brother-in-law and sister-in-law in the front seat tried to comfort us during the trip by talking. The three of us sat silently in the back seat. Our thoughts and our feelings could not fit into words.

Arriving at the large hospital, we were taken to a room to wait for the doctor's report. A short time later a physician came to give us a prognosis on Karen. She was in a deep coma from the severe head injury, not breathing on her own, and unresponsive to all stimuli. She was "clinically silent." Brain scans had been taken, and they were flat. More scans would be performed later to see if there was any change, but the outlook wasn't good. We were informed that our daughter's life was being temporarily sustained by the assistance of machines. Drugs administered through the vein were keeping her heart beating and maintaining her blood pressure, and a respirator was pumping oxygen into her lungs.

Although the doctor was trying to gently tell us Karen's condition was terminal, I could not accept what he was saying. With my ears I listened to him speaking the words, but with my heart I could not hear him. Staring at me strangely, the doctor asked, "Do you understand what I am saying, Mrs. Sawyers?" Although I could hear myself answering, "Yes," I found it hard to believe I was actually speaking. How could I utter a word that signified the collapse of our world?

Taken to another waiting room near Intensive Care, we continued the unbearable waiting. Many of Karen's friends joined us at the hospital to await news of her condition; we were glad they were there for support. That evening and the following days were a blur of faces and embraces as our family and our friends sought to comfort us.

As we waited for visiting in ICU, many questions came to torture me: Why had this senseless calamity befallen our little one? Why did it have to be Karen? It seemed unfair! Karen was so beautiful, her life so full of hope and promise. Was life being stolen from her just as she was beginning to blossom and to taste life's joys?

The three of us were finally allowed into Intensive Care to see Karen. My daughter's chest moved up and down as the mechanical respirator breathed for her. She was comatose and made no spontaneous movements; her eyes were partially open and staring. A nurse explained that everything possible was being done for our daughter. I looked down upon my precious daughter's motionless body. Taking her hand, I softly spoke to her, "I love you, Karen. We all love you." We all spoke loving words as if she were listening. There was no response as Karen continued to lie still and lifeless. She appeared withdrawn from life.

Day and night merged into a blur as we continued our sad vigil. Questions concerning my daughter filled me with mental anguish: Does she know anything that is going on? What if she is suffering and can't tell me. Oh, how could our family bear this torment? Longing to escape the mental torture, I wished to be home so I could just run down the road and scream. Would it help to be able to do that? Where was my help? What was my help?

As we continued to wait, my thoughts retreated to the previous holidays to the night when Karen and I had decided to read to one another while the men watched football on television. Snuggled under the covers, we read several articles before coming to the condensed version of the book, *Song for Sarah*, a series of letters written by Paula D'Arcy for her daughter, Sarah. D'Arcy began her letters in 1973 when she learned that she was pregnant with her daughter. She writes, "I little guessed then that within two and a half years they [the letters] would be my detailed recollection of a time and a life that were suddenly and unkindly ended."[1] D'Arcy's husband and small daughter were later killed in a tragic accident.

Thinking back to the time when Karen and I had read the account, I remembered telling her I didn't think I could bear it if a tragedy like that ever happened to us. Karen had said, "Mom, you would have to." Only a little over two months had passed since our reading of the account of Mrs. D'Arcy's sorrow. Now, a similar misfortune was happening to my own family. In the midst of my grief, there was no way I could know that God was planning to use the D'Arcy article in another way in my life, that in the future God would use the same article to direct me to a man who would be a witness to me in the dark night of my soul.

On Saturday we conferred again with the neurologist. "I'm sorry to have to tell you that the head scan shows no improvement," he said. "The readings are flat. Another scan will be taken tomorrow to see if there is any change. If there is no change, after the period of time required by law, your daughter should be taken off the machines maintaining life functions. To leave her on the life-supporting machines would only prolong her present condition artificially. Medically we have done all we can. We don't expect you to make the decision; after the prescribed period of time has passed, we will decide."

My emotions screamed inside me. How could doctors talk in a way that seemed so impersonal? He was talking about my daughter, my little girl, who had laughed and loved only hours before. Now, she was in a coma, her languid body motionless as the doctors decided what to do. But I couldn't fault the physicians; I knew they cared despite their terminology.

By Saturday night we were totally exhausted; we had not slept since our daughter's accident. That night, lounging in the waiting room, we did manage a little fitful sleep. Often during that long night, I awoke to go through all the "if-onlys": if-only we had told Karen that she couldn't cut her friend's hair; if-only we had told her not to ride on the boy's motorcycle; if-only we could turn back the clock and make this stop; if-only...

We had always been so careful with our children, never taking chances on their health or their safety. When they were sick, we immediately took them to the doctor. Once David had broken his foot, and Karen had hurt her knee in sports. We took both to specialists where they received the finest care. Now, after all the years of care and concern, this horrible tragedy had happened to our daughter.

Two days had passed since our daughter's tragic accident. It was Sunday morning, March 7, 1982. It was so hard to live. I didn't know how my mind could tolerate the seemingly unbearable shock of our little girl's situation. That morning Karen's physicians had informed us there was no hope for her recovery. It was apparent to them that our daughter's brain had been irreversibly damaged. Karen had lost her higher brain functions; she could no longer think, she could no longer feel. In other words, Karen was no longer Karen. And, the doctors said, Karen never would be again.

Medically, our daughter was existing on machines. We knew Karen wouldn't want such a condition to continue. The feisty, fun-loving girl we had known and loved for fifteen years would not want any part of that sort of helpless existence. For Karen's sake the doctor's felt that the best thing to do was to cease artificial life-support. Further treatment was hopeless. We had to let go of our Karen; we had to let our beloved daughter die in peace.

PROFOUND GRIEF

As I awoke the following morning, the realization washed over me like a tidal wave that my daughter was gone. My inner-most being felt despair as waves of sorrow engulfed me. From that moment each new day meant facing the paradox of the unfaceable, awakening each morning to the reality of what had happened to Karen.

Our house screamed of Karen's absence. The void was almost palpable, the air thick with sorrow and with uncertainty. From the moment we first arrived home from the hospital after Karen's death, we didn't know how to handle our grief. We were all hurting so badly. How could we go on living and breathing with all this hurt?

It seemed that the world should stop, but I knew it wouldn't. While I felt incapable of going on with life, the rest of the world was moving on as usual. People everywhere were enjoying their everyday lives, but our world was upside down. As we drove to the funeral home to make final arrangements, vehicles such as garbage and milk trucks whizzed up and down the road, reminding us that life was continuing.

Sadly, we made the preparations for our daughter's funeral. With great care we planned each detail. On Tuesday, March 9, 1982, with broken hearts, we buried our dear daughter. No words can express the inward misery we felt.

In the sorrowful days following Karen's death, it was not easy for me to see things realistically. Wasn't there some way to bend events to make this stop? Couldn't things be reversed somehow to restore the past? If only this were just a nightmare that would soon end. But it wasn't a bad dream; it was reality. Karen was gone. What a terrible finality! Everything seemed futile and hopeless. There was no answer, no way of straightening it out.

I missed Karen. I wanted to see my girl, to put my arms around her, to hold her near. Sometimes, longing for her presence, I went into her room and hugged one of her sweaters close; what else could I do?

I was nearly paralyzed by my grief; it took an extreme effort of will for me to function at the simplest level. My legs dragged as I mechanically went through the motions of cooking, cleaning, and laundry washing. Shakily, I proceeded through each task, summoning up just enough energy to do the chores which just had to be done.

Seriously considering withdrawing from society and hiding at home, I dreaded having to face people all day at my salon. Yet I knew that contact with others would compel me to cope with life at least on a surface level. If I stayed home, I had no idea what might happen. So, two weeks after my daughter's death, I returned to work at my shop. Apprehension filled me each morning as I thought of facing my tasks. I didn't know how I could perform my duties because I had so much trouble concentrating. From the moment I had seen Karen lying unconscious on the street after the accident, I had suffered from a sensation similar to a stupor. This vacant, numb sensation stayed with me for months. As daily affairs occurred around me, it was difficult for me to tune in or to communicate.

My customers went out of their way to offer me the sympathy and understanding that I needed to survive at work. Nevertheless, it was difficult for me to appear interested and attentive in what was going on around me. As customers chatted with me, I hoped I was nodding at the correct times and saying the right things. I was too preoccupied to be good company. By the end of each day, I was exhausted from the struggle to maintain a pretense of alertness.

Struggling with a barrage of emotions — grief, anger, frustration, confusion, bitterness — I found it difficult to be alert to everyday affairs. Feeling bitter toward Karen's doctors, I wondered if they had really told us the truth about her condition. Did we make a mistake in believing them? Months later, when I was thinking more clearly, I realized that Karen's physicians had not been trying to deceive us. After reading a book which thoroughly explained how doctors determine the extent of brain damage after injuries, I understood that my daughter's physicians had done the right thing in removing her life support systems.

I also blamed myself for Karen's absence. Her death went against the most basic of my parental instincts. After all, a mother's first task is to preserve the safety of her child. It seemed my fault that Karen had died because I was responsible for her as a parent. Yet I couldn't save her. It was months before I could see that these were irrational thoughts, that I was blaming myself needlessly.

And, I felt bitter toward God. This wasn't fair at all! I couldn't think of another girl any prettier or sweeter than Karen. She had so much potential. As I thought of my daughter's hopes and plans for the future, my heart overflowed with grief. If God really existed and cared, why didn't he allow Karen to go on with her life?

On the other hand, if there was no God, life was purposeless. What was the reason for living if this tragic world was all there was to our existence? Entangled in a seemingly hopeless quandary, I was desperately searching for answers to the perplexing questions which were troubling me. Surely there was more to this than met the eye, but, if so, where were the answers? I didn't know how I could continue to live with all the uncertainty.

For even a moment, I couldn't escape from my sorrow or from my confusion. The normal, healthy "escapes" which I had relied on all my life were suddenly stolen from me. I found it impossible to become absorbed in a book or in television because my attention span had become so short. Feeling disassociated from my surroundings and from the concerns of the world, I found it difficult to carry on an ordinary conversation. Little details of life now were so insipid. In fact, nothing really seemed very important anymore. It was difficult to show interest in hearing about someone's Tupperware party or the latest gossip because I simply didn't care. I realized, however, that I needed to feign interest in the things going on around me for the sake of others. Food no longer attracted me because my appetite was gone; it was difficult for me to even consume an entire sandwich. While other people were on diets, I was losing weight without even trying.

Sleep wasn't an escape either. Dozing off to sleep at night, I intermittently woke up with a start, with an empty feeling in the pit of my stomach. Night and day, the realization of the loss of my daughter weighed heavily upon my mind.

In my worst moments, I panicked. I worried that the quicksand of my grief would pull me farther and farther down until I lost my mind. I longed to flee, to somehow excape from the pain of my loss. But life did not spare me. There was no way to disengage from the suffering.

Karen's death had unbalanced all the relationships of our lives within our immediate family and with all the people who were important to us. The patterns of our life together did not work anymore; everything was out of kilter. Karen was, we had believed, to have filled a place in our lives until the end of our days. Now, that space was empty. She would have grown up, become an adult, perhaps married and had children of her own. It seemed an affront, a reversal of nature, that she had died before us.

As a family we each carried our mourning in individual ways; the stages of our grief and the expressions of our sorrow were different. After the first few months, we talked very little about Karen's death or about the effect it had on us. Our emotions were hidden inside. I felt a need to communicate, to remember and talk about her life, to look at her pictures and physical articles, but other family members could not talk of Karen easily. Not wanting to alienate my own family, I tried to refrain from broaching the subject.

Many other people missed Karen as well. The most poignant reminder of this came over one year after her death. I was babysitting for a young couple, friends of ours, while they attended her father's funeral. When Karen was alive, she had frequently babysat for the couple's small boys, Troy and Tyler. She loved both boys but was especially captivated by Tyler, the youngest. The day we babysat with the boys, Tyler asked me to read to him and followed me into Karen's room to help get the books which were in a bottom dresser drawer. Tyler was only about one year and nine months old when Karen was killed, and I didn't think he still remembered her. But, as Tyler and I walked into her bedroom, he turned to me and sadly said, "Karen's gone."

Surprised that he still remembered her, I asked gently, "Do you miss Karen?"

Tyler answered, "I miss Karen."

ONE SWEET DAY

A friend of ours who lost a son sent us the book, *The Bereaved Parent,* by Harriet Sarnoff Schiff. Books of this type and association with other parents who had lost children were my biggest emotional help. We began attending meetings for bereaved parents, and this also provided support. When a person is hurting, he needs others who understand what he is experiencing. Healing balm is contained in the sincerely spoken words: "I know how you feel." I soon recognized, however, that I needed more than emotional help. I was hungry for spiritual guidance.

It continued to be difficult for me to function at everyday tasks while searching for seemingly unobtainable answers about life: Why did this terrible tragedy happen to my daughter? How did God fit into the picture? Was there really a God who cared? Anxiety over profound questions of this type tore at my soul night and day. Few moments of consciousness existed for me that my mind was not churning these uncertainties over and over.

But where could I find help? Finally, the realization dawned on me that perhaps I could pray to God for help with this problem. If there really was a God, surely He would help me find answers. Three months after Karen's death, I got up from bed one night at 3:00 a.m. to ask for help in understanding. In desperation I prayed that God, if he was really "there," would help me in my search for spiritual truth.

Perhaps the case of the Ethiopian nobleman from Acts 8 will further explain my dilemma. While reading the Old Testament, the Ethiopian came to the book of Isaiah. Unable to understand what the prophet Isaiah meant, the nobleman needed someone to interpret the Scripture to him. Aware that the Ethiopian was a sincere searcher, God sent an angel to instruct Philip to interpret the Scripture for him and to lead him to a saving knowledge of Jesus Christ. Likewise, God knew I was a sincere searcher. Many basic, unanswered questions remained in my mind, yet I was sincerely trying to search for truth.

A most remarkable thing happened the afternoon after my prayer for spiritual help. Previously I told about Karen and me reading together the *Reader's Digest* version of *Song for Sarah* by Paula D'Arcy. Soon after Karen's death, I bought the book version. I had noticed the preliminaries of *Song for Sarah* included an endorsement by a man named Sheldon Vanauken who was extolling the value of Mrs. D'Arcy's book.

I mention this because of something which happened later the same day of my prayer for spiritual guidance. Deciding to go shopping at the large mall of a nearby city, I found my curiosity aroused when I "accidentally" noticed the book, *A Severe Mercy*, by Sheldon Vanauken, the man I just mentioned. Under the name of the book and the author were these words: "Includes eighteen previously unpublished letters by C. S. Lewis." Although I had never heard of C. S. Lewis, I assumed he must be someone very famous and important. Later, spying a book by this author, I impulsively decided to purchase both books.

Back at home reading the two books that night, I was totally amazed. Vanauken explained in his book how he and his wife went through a search for spiritual truth and answers. Corresponding with C. S. Lewis, Vanauken asked many philosophical questions about Christianity, and C. S. Lewis answered the questions by letter. It was remarkable that the Vanaukens asked C. S. Lewis some of the same questions that had been troubling me.

For example, in *A Severe Mercy,* Vanauken asked C. S. Lewis the question of whether Christianity is the only true religion. In an excerpt from a letter written by him, Vanauken observes, "Very simply, it seems to me that some intelligent power made this universe and that all men must know it, axiomatically, and must feel awe at the power's infiniteness. It seems to me natural that men, knowing and feeling so, should attempt to elaborate on that simplicity . . . and so arose the world's religions. But how can just one of them be singled out as true?"[3]

As I read C. S. Lewis' clear answers to this and other questions, and as I later read his numerous books, Christianity started making sense to me. C. S. Lewis was the first Christian I had ever encountered who shared how he had "thought through" or "reasoned" his beliefs. Reading his books, I could see real answers did exist to problem questions about Christianity.

The second book I purchased that day was C. S. Lewis' book, *A Grief Observed*, a personal narrative describing in vivid detail the author's experience of intense grief and mental anguish suffered after the death of his wife. The couple had only been married a short time before her death, so he openly questioned why God had allowed her untimely departure. As I read his contemplative plaint on the sensations of heart felt grief and sincere questions, I felt less alone. Here was someone who not only understood the dilemma of uncertainties and doubts, but who also knew the misery of deep sorrow.

Reading the epilogue, I was amazed that C. S. Lewis had felt God calling him to become a Christian. Explaining the long route of C. S. Lewis' conversion, Chad Walsh writes that C. S. Lewis had perceived God's presence through events triggered by such things as "a bar of music, a landscape, a forgotten memory. The experience is an instantaneous sense of seeing into the heart of things, as though a universe beyond the universe opened itself wide for an instant and as instantly slammed its doors shut."[4] I immediately recognized the various descriptions of these experiences which C. S. Lewis had encountered and named "Joy."

After Karen's death, despite my heartache and confusion, at certain times I could deeply feel the presence and the love of God. My natural senses were sometimes heightened in an odd manner which transcended the limits of ordinary consciousness: sunsets seemed to surround me in an aura of light of almost unbearable beauty; lovely music had a sublime quality which was nearly heavenly. At such times, I felt the presence of God calling and drawing me to Himself.

In numerous ways I had deeply sensed God's love and concern for me, but the most wonderful instance occurred in a profound way that will live in my heart forever. I was returning home in my car from a visit to a nearby town. Driving down the road, my thoughts on Karen, I heard a girl with a melodious voice singing a bittersweet song on the radio. This was a song I had never heard before and have never heard again since that time. Tears streamed down my face as she sang, "I'll see you again one sweet day." Suddenly a strange thing happened. For some unknown reason, I momentarily glanced up at clouds stirring in the sky, and in that moment, within my spirit, I felt God's presence comforting me and assuring me that the message of the song was personally true — that I was going to see Karen again "one sweet day."

Thinking back over everything that happened, I realized that events had been more than coincidental. I thought about the strange way the book *Song for Sarah* had led me to a book by Sheldon Vanauken, and how that book, in turn, had directed me to books by C. S. Lewis, the great Christian writer and apologist. It was not by mere chance that I had discovered those books. Without a doubt, I knew God had provided assistance in my search for spiritual truth. I had asked God for help in my search for answers, and He had answered my prayer. Finally receiving the spiritual guidance I so desperately needed, I accepted Christ as my Lord and Savior in the summer of 1982.

As a new Christian, my spiritual needs had been met. What I needed now was to incorporate the loss of my daughter into my life so I could become emotionally whole again. It was tough, and it took years of struggle, but I succeeded in rebuilding my life. I was able to meet my daughter's death on its own anguishing terms, grieve over it, ask questions, and allow it to become a part of my life's complex pattern.

So what makes this book unique is that it is written by someone who has experienced what you are now experiencing, the loss of a child. Although competent doctors and psychiatrists have written many books about the grieving process, this book has been written by someone who understands how you feel.

In the pages that follow, I will provide you with appropriate ways for coping with grief so that you, too, can rebuild your life. At this point you may feel, like I once did, that there is no escape from grief. Yet I escaped. It didn't happen overnight. It took many years of prayer and interaction with family, friends, and professionals to cope with the loss. But I did survive, and in this book, I will share with you some ways in which you, too, can survive your own child's death.

The suggestions provided in this book are drawn from both my own personal experience and the expertise of many doctors, professors, and others who have studied the grief process. They are organized into 10 chapters that roughly parallel what experts call the stages of grieving:

1   Surviving Shock and Denial
2   Surviving Emotional Suffering
3   Surviving Depression
4   Surviving Panic
5   Surviving Guilt
6   Surviving Anger
7   Surviving Physical Aspects of Grief
8   Surviving Life Changes
9   Engaging in Meaningful Activity
10 Affirming Reality

Yes, you can survive. We all have a capacity to grieve in ways that integrate loss into our lives over the course of time. When you attend to the painful spiritual and emotional wounds present in your life, as time passes you will begin to find hope. And, as you gently bring hope for survival into your life each day, your broken heart will slowly begin to mend and to feel joy and happiness again.

Of course, I cannot guarantee that reading this book will help everyone. But my prayer is that some of my suggestions will provide comfort to you and help heal your soul.

Norma Sawyers-Kurz
Summer 2014

*The Lord is near
to the brokenhearted
and saves those who are
crushed in spirit.*

— Psalm 34:18

1

Surviving Shock and Denial

When your child dies, you can feel as if your whole life has been shattered and nothing will ever be the same. Whether your loss came unexpectedly or after a long-term illness, you and your family are likely to experience shock and denial, according to experts on death and dying. You will find it difficult to accept the fact that it happened.

Such sorrow, experts say, often "anesthetizes" us, preventing us from having to face the grim reality all at once. In other words, we know intellectually that our child has died, but emotionally we don't want to believe it, so unconsciously we set barriers in the way, making complete acceptance a slow process. Shock and denial give us time to accustom ourselves to the terrible facts.

The shock and denial stage may last anywhere from a few minutes to a few days or weeks.[1] But it happens to most people. And contrary to popular belief, this stage is a good thing. It offers a temporary mental escape that sustains us until we are emotionally ready to move on to the next stage of grief.

ASK FOR ASSISTANCE IN DEALING WITH DETAILS SUCH AS FUNERAL ARRANGEMENTS

When we are numb with shock, everyday activities of life can seem like enormous tasks. It can take all of our strength, for example, just to take care of our physical needs, such as food preparation and grooming. More complex tasks, like making funeral arrangements, are even more daunting.

In *Surviving Grief ... and Learning to Live Again*, Catherine M. Sanders, a psychologist specializing in bereavement, notes that "the rituals of death require a lot from us, not the least of which is that first awful, wrenching trip to the funeral home to make the arrangements."[2] She adds that at a time when we feel least prepared for decision making, we are bombarded with numerous questions, leaving us feeling overwhelmed.

If you find that taking care of these responsibilities or even thinking clearly is difficult, enlist the assistance of friends or relatives. Most of the people closest to you would like to lend a hand, so let them know how they can aid you during this extremely difficult early period. Perhaps you need assistance for such tasks as writing the obituary, answering the phone, preparing the meals, and so forth. Don't be ashamed to ask or receive much-needed help with these tasks.

ACCEPT EMOTIONAL SUPPORT FROM FRIENDS, RELATIVES, AND OTHER PARENTS

The heartache and pain associated with losing your child is so traumatic that just getting up in the morning to face the day can be a challenge. To help you through this process, accept emotional support from friends and relatives. In addition to loyalty, they provide love and sympathy and can help you share the pain. Talk to them.

Don't be disappointed, however, if some friends or relatives don't know what to say. People often have difficulty expressing themselves well or reaching out to each other during times of grief. Some people will lift you up with their encouraging words. Others have more difficulty expressing their support. In addition, be aware that some friends or relatives may avoid you during this time or refuse to talk about the tragedy for fear that it may bring either you or them too much grief.

Other parents who have lost a child can be another source of emotional support. Of course, your loss is unique, so no one else can say that they know exactly how you feel or what you are going through. But other parents who have experienced a loss are in a better position to understand what you are going through. Seek them out and share your story with them.

In fact, you may want to join a support group of other parents who have lost children. In *How to Go on Living When Someone You Love Dies*, bereavement specialist Therese A. Rando writes that "self-help groups can be wonderfully therapeutic in assisting you with your mourning."[3] She says that support groups not only provide us with encouragement, they also provide practical suggestions for dealing with grief. These groups can fill a gap when we find that others avoid us.[4]

Don't expect that any one person will have all the insight and compassion you are craving in your personal loss. But do take whatever emotional support you can from those who have experienced the loss of a child. In the midst of your sorrow, know too that "the Lord is near to the brokenhearted and saves those who are crushed in spirit" (Psalm 34:18).

SEEK GUIDANCE FROM A MINISTER OR SKILLED COUNSELOR

In his book *Healing Your Grieving Heart: 100 Practical Ideas*, Alan D. Wolfelt says that "while grief counseling is not for everyone, many individuals are helped through their grief journeys by a compassionate counselor."[5] He advises that, if possible, you should locate a counselor experienced in dealing with grief and loss issues. He adds that your pastor also may be a good source of counsel, but only if he or she understands your need to mourn your loss and to search for meaning.

This doesn't mean that parents who lose a child shouldn't talk to friends or relatives. But a pastor or counselor usually has more knowledge and resources to help you work through emotions like anger and guilt. They also can validate your loss and provide a frame of reference as to what constitutes "healthy" mourning. Some people also prefer the safety and security of a therapeutic environment.

In addition to ministers and psychologists, other resources include: crisis centers that focus on coping with tragedy and sorrow; groups that deal with working through the grief process; and capable church leaders who are trained to handle unresolved emotional disturbances.

WRITE YOUR FEELINGS IN A JOURNAL

Writing is another way of releasing emotions during the early stages of grief. You can begin by attempting to answer the questions you have been asking yourself over and over again. "Why did this happen?" "How can I go on?"

You also may have feelings or thoughts you wish you had shared with your child while he or she was still alive. Rando says, "Although you cannot have the actual interaction with your loved one ... there are ways that you can deal with unfinished business. ... Sometimes writing a letter to your loved one can be therapeutic."[6]

Write a letter in your journal to your child. Pour out your heart. Express your love and say all the things you wish you had said. Identify any unfinished business or unresolved emotional issues in the relationship with your child, and then write down the words you wish you had said. "I love you," or "I'm sorry," or "I needed you."

Of course, you may also be questioning God's sovereignty in a world where illness and tragedy so often strike. Don't be afraid to tell the Lord all about it as you write in your journal.

BE GENTLE AND KIND TO YOURSELF

If you're like most people who lose a child, you are probably wondering how you will ever learn to go on with the rest of your life. But with the support of family, friends, and God, you can nurture yourself into believing once again in your life. Note that I said "nurture," because overcoming grief doesn't happen in days, weeks, or even months. It usually takes years for many parents to integrate the death of a child into the fabric of their lives.

Pay close attention to your emotional well-being.[7] You are emotionally vulnerable right now, so don't beat yourself up for any action, deed, or word from the past. The past is gone, so the best thing to do now is to focus on the future and on your eventual recovery.

Concentrate on your physical well-being as well. When grief is intense, the body uses up vast amounts of physical energy. Nancy O'Connor, author of *Letting Go With Love: The Grieving Process*, says we should go easy on ourselves during early grief, because "mental confusion and low energy levels are very common. Fatigue and exhaustion result from both expending the energy to cope and resisting the emotional responses that continue to surface."[8]

It is vitally important at this time for you to get proper nutrition and the best rest you can. Don't overdo it. Your most special need right now is to be gentle and kind to yourself.

CARRY ON WITH ACTIVITIES AS MUCH AS POSSIBLE

It is good for us to keep fairly busy with our usual daily activities during the first stage of grief. Although we may need help with some tasks early on, it is certainly not good to become completely dependent on others or to let them make all our decisions for us. There is therapeutic value in doing things for ourselves because this will help most of us come out of the shock phase and into the grief process.

Staying busy is good because it also helps prevent us from dwelling too much on painful memories. In her book, *How to Survive the Loss of a Child*, Sanders says that "the search for some meaning in a child's death is an ongoing rumination for survivors. It is as if we must unearth every detail surrounding the death, so we can begin to piece together this incomprehensible tragedy."[9]

Intense thinking about the circumstances surrounding the death of a child is a natural response to the loss and a reflection of the internal grief. However, preoccupation with thoughts about the death can become obsessive. At those times, when our minds are running in circles, there are steps we can take to fix our minds on more pleasant thoughts.

First, we can recognize that memories can seem more profound in certain situations, and we can try to discover ways to stop these images in their tracks. The "triggers" that evoke these painful memories may be something like shopping in a particular store, driving down a certain stretch of roadway, dining in a particular restaurant, and so forth. After you identify these triggers, avoid them as much as possible, at least for the time-being.

Another way of overcoming painful memories is to look at the circumstances from a different perspective. This is sometimes called looking for the "silver lining in every cloud," a powerful way to keep our minds from dwelling too much on the anguish we feel and to bring us peace in the midst of the storm.

Although negative and painful thoughts will continue to occur from time to time, you don't have to keep entertaining them. It will be difficult, but you can consciously make an effort to focus your mind on the good things in your life. You can do as Scripture tells us and concentrate on whatever is true, honorable, right, pure, lovely, or good in your life, and let your mind dwell on those things (See Philippians 4:8).

TRY TO FACE THE REALITY OF YOUR LOSS AS THE SHOCK BEGINS TO WANE

When a child dies, we, as parents, reason that such sorrow happens to other people, but it can't be happening in our lives. Shock forces us to retreat mentally until a later time, when we can get a grip on the reality of our loss.

The length of time we remain stuck in shock varies. This stage can last for an incredibly long time if we refuse to face reality and to deal with our grief. To remain in this stage for weeks or even months most likely means that a person is suffering from unhealthy grief. So, as shock begins to wane, it is vitally important you allow yourself to face the reality of your loss and to begin to process all of the emotions you are feeling.

Wolfelt writes, "this requires that we embrace the pain of our loss — something we naturally don't want to do. It is easier to avoid, repress, or push away the pain of grief than it is to confront it."[10] Although the only way you can address your grief is by facing the pain, you will probably need to embrace your pain in small "doses," because you could not survive if you were to experience all the pain at once.

READ INSPIRATIONAL MATERIALS FOR SOLACE AND EMOTIONAL RELEASE

Another way of obtaining solace or emotional release is to read works of poetry, written from either a secular or a religious perspective. Poetry achieves its effects by rhythm, sound patterns, imagery and a loftiness of tone that not only provides comfort, but also brings, for some people, a release of emotions through crying. This can be especially helpful to bereaved parents in early grief because denial and shock sometimes prevent us from experiencing the intensity of our emotions or from shedding tears.

Along with secular writings, you might want to turn to books of the Bible, such as the Psalms, for poetic encouragement. Write down scriptures that provide comfort and keep them handy for future reference. When you find it difficult to go on, struggle with the agony of loss, or need a word of encouragement, pick up your list of Scriptures.

*Hope in God,
for I shall again
praise Him, the help
of my countenance,
and my God.*

— Psalm 43:5

2

Surviving Emotional Suffering

After going through the shock-and-denial stage, experts say that most people enter the second stage of grief, which involves emotional suffering and loneliness. As a bereaved parent, you face the possibility, however, that you may find yourself reverting back and forth among stages or totally skipping some phases of the grief process.[1]

Don't be upset with yourself if, for example, you find yourself temporarily going back into shock even after you think you are well past this stage. There are fleeting moments when we see beyond our numbness and begin to acknowledge our loss. There are other times when reality seems too horrific, and we deny it hopelessly. After what seems an interminable period of struggle along this pathway, you eventually will accept your child's death.

ALLOW YOURSELF TO PROCESS THE EMOTIONS YOU ARE FEELING

As shock begins to wear off, you are finally able to feel the intensity of your grief and move into the second phase of grieving. The insulation of the first phase is gone and you are left feeling raw and painfully exposed. You may experience a wide range of emotions, including anger, guilt, frustration, fear, panic, and despair.

But Rando explains that "feeling and expressing your emotions is one of the most critical requirements of grief. If you do not find an acceptable way to express all your feelings of grief, you will not be able to resolve it."[2]

Right now you may not be able to identify all your feelings over the loss and its consequences. But the important thing is that you need to allow yourself to express your emotions. Your method does not necessarily matter as long as you release your feelings and do not cause harm to yourself or others.

The emotional suffering a bereaved parent experiences is an indescribable, gut-wrenching agony of enormous severity. Yet we realize that the only way to come out on the other side of this pain is to embrace it, to go toward it, and then to travel through it.

GIVE YOURSELF PERMISSION TO CRY

The expression of grief is a natural part of our human experience. Yet we somehow get the idea that the tears of grief are out of place in our modern world. Society implies that crying is somehow "bad" for us and tries to remove our natural and healthy expressions of sorrow by replacing them with expressions such as: "Be a man!" or "Dry up those tears!"

But it's ok to cry. James R. White, who wrote *Grief: Our Path Back to Peace*, observes that "men are often ashamed by the emotions they feel when grieving, but there is no reason for shame. God made us feeling beings, and we dare not shortchange ourselves simply because our society has a very unrealistic view of what it means to be a 'man.'"[3]

A world without emotions would be a cold, indifferent place where there would be no appreciation of the wonder of a rainbow, the majesty of a sunrise, or the beauty of a mountain range. There would be no feelings of joy when a baby is born and no exuberance when something momentous occurs. Our lives would be bland; we would be like robots just going through the motions.

When God gave us emotions, He knew what He was doing. He gave us the ability to laugh, but He also gave us the ability to cry. Thus He is the One to whom we can always turn when we need to unload our feelings. Whether we are ranting and raving or crying and wailing, He can patiently handle it all. Go to Him in prayer, seek His face, ask Him to show you helpful scriptures, and request His help through the ministry of the Holy Spirit.

REMEMBER HAPPY MOMENTS

One aspect of the emotional suffering stage involves our bittersweet remembrances of the past. We recall memories of events which occurred before the loss of our child, and they often bring us to tears.

A way to combat the melancholy nature of memories is to make a positive experience out of your recollections. Go get the family photo album you've been hiding away, bring it out, open the pages, and change your negative remembrances into a positive experience as you recall the memories brought back by those old photos. Your tears will flow for sure, but why not allow some joyful tears as you dwell on uplifting thoughts about your child's accomplishments, personality, or unique human traits?

Actively remember the special qualities of the child who has died, and commemorate in your heart the life that was lived. Remember the joy of knowing them and the contributions they made during their lifetime. In this way you are not only preventing your memories from becoming disabling, but you are benefiting from the therapeutic value in recalling happy memories. In the process you will become empowered as you take charge of the quality of your memories rather than letting the memories take charge of you.

Another way to fight off the negative aspect of remembrances is to realize that the same God who gave us a beautiful yesterday will bring us an equally fulfilling tomorrow. In this way, we can begin to move from despair to hope as we gain a new understanding of the past and a fresh vision of the future. For if God gave us a yesterday that was so full meaning, then why not a meaningful tomorrow?

COMBAT LONELINESS BY SHOPPING, RUNNING ERRANDS, OR CORRESPONDING WITH OTHERS

For bereaved parents, the feelings of isolation and loneliness associated with losing a child can be overwhelming. When you find yourself alone in your despair, you need to find ways to reduce your isolation. Westberg advises that mourners should not remain alone in their grief, because "we all need the warm affection and encouragement of those about us. As we are the recipients of such affection, it makes it easier for us to sense that our present attitude of shutting out all new opportunities for meaningful living is unrealistic."[4]

For example, you can combat feelings of isolation by doing such things as going shopping or running errands. Go to the nearest mall, wander through the various stores, and visit with salespersons or strike up conversations with other shoppers as they lounge in waiting areas such as food courts. Or invent errands, like paying your local bills in person instead of mailing. Find whatever excuses you can to get yourself propelled away from the isolation of your home.

When we are unable to actually be with someone else, we can also compensate by correspondence through letters, email, or telephone. Sharing your feelings with friends through written words can be very therapeutic. You will be most fortunate if you can find a pen pal who shows sensitivity, responds quickly, and remains steadfast in corresponding with you through letters or email. One advantage of written correspondence is that it can be done at any time of the day or night. Keep in mind that when you correspond with others through written or spoken words, the possibility always exists that they will say something painful or discouraging. People often make klutzy mistakes, so don't be angry, but just forgive the person and search elsewhere for a more understanding person among your friends.

Never forget, however, that at times when friends and family fail to provide the support you need, there is one friend who will never fail you, who will never desert you, and who will never change, "Jesus Christ, the same yesterday and today, yes and forever" (Hebrews 13:8).

TAKE CARE OF YOUR HEALTH

When you are experiencing the pain and loneliness of the loss of your child, the danger exists that you may respond in ways that can adversely impact your health, such as abusing drugs or alcohol or other chemicals. People who abuse these substances face a serious risk of becoming dependent or addicted to them, because with increased use the amount of the drug needed to dull the pain escalates and the severity of the reaction to substance withdrawal increases.

In addition to the risk of possible addiction and the destruction of brain cells, the use of alcohol and other drugs can delay the grieving process. You avoid accepting reality.

Of course, a more serious side effect of using drugs is an increased risk of committing suicide to avoid emotional suffering. The thought of suicide may be the desperate reaction of a parent to incredible feelings of hopelessness or despair brought on by the seeming lack of positive solutions to the dilemma of the loss of a child. Dr O'Connor emphasizes that in cases such as this, suicide can be "a reaction to incredible stress, fear, and depression, an act of desperation. It is not a rational 'action,' but a 'reaction' to [what is perceived to be] an intolerable circumstance currently operating in the life of a person."[5]

Suicide has often been referred to as the ultimate cry for help. If you have been contemplating suicide or someone you love has been giving verbal or non-verbal clues about self-destruction, contact your local Suicide Prevention Service immediately. Don't wait! Suicidal behavior should always be taken very seriously.

Most cities in the United States have crisis intervention centers (names may vary in different locales) where people can call to talk to caring people trained in suicide prevention. They can talk you through the immediate crisis, refer you to competent counseling, or console a suicidal family member.

Refuse to dwell on a negative picture of your circumstances. God's picture is one of healing, recovery, and restoration. Although at times you may feel like giving up, always "hope in God" (See Psalm 43:5).

REMEMBER YOU ARE NOT ALONE

You may reach a point where you feel withdrawn from God. Something seems to come in between God and yourself so that you feel an awful sense of separation from Him. You may even think that God doesn't care or that He has deserted you. It is here that you may cry out bitter words from the depths of your soul, such as: "Where are you God?" "I hurt so terribly!" "Why don't You help me?"

What you long for most from God is immediate answers to all your troubling questions and quick assurance that everything will be alright again. But that is not the way our sovereign Lord works. Nowhere in Scripture does God promise you a shortcut through the valley or a quick resolution to your grief. What He does promise is supernatural strength to those who trust and wait for Him (See Isaiah 40:31). While God will not immediately remove your sorrow, He will sustain and strengthen you as you travel through your ordeal.

In *A Grief Observed*, C.S. Lewis writes that "you can't see anything clearly when your vision is blurred with tears."[6] What a true statement! How often we are unable to catch a glimpse of God when tears of grief cloud over our eyes.

But let me assure you: no matter how forsaken you think you are, or how alone you may feel, you are not alone. Even if you do not feel God's presence, He is near. Wherever you may be, God is there also. His omnipresence surrounds you, watches over you, and embraces you. If you do not feel His presence, ask Him to make His presence real. Then begin to take comfort in His attendant mercy and grace in your life as you gain new peace, strength, and hope for the future.

*I would have despaired
unless I believed [to] see the
goodness of the Lord in
the land of the living.*

— Psalm 27:13

3

Surviving Depression

Following the death of a child, parents often find themselves slipping into the depths of despair. Judith R. Bernstein, author of *When the Bough Breaks: Forever After the Death of a Son or Daughter*, emphasizes the traumatic quality of the loss: "When a child dies, the very ground on which we depend for stability heaves and quakes and the rightness and orderliness of our existence are destroyed. The loss of a child is shattering, unique among losses."[1]

Although we may grieve deeply for the loss of an aged parent, relative, or friend, the predictability of the universe remains intact, for we understand the mortality of elderly persons. But when a child dies, the order of nature is thrown askew and our world is turned upside down. It isn't surprising then that many bereaved mothers and fathers may suffer from depression.

DON'T BE ASHAMED IF YOU BECOME DEPRESSED

Depression is an affliction which can be as mild as a "blue mood" which leaves you feeling temporarily sad, or as severe as clinical depression which can lead to hospitalization. Mild depression is a common reaction to significant loss and a normal part of the grief process. A bereaved parent may lack energy or motivation, feel helpless, hopeless or powerless, or experience a myriad of other emotional symptoms often associated with depression. If you are feeling blue or depressed, just remember that it's a normal part of the grieving process.

But deep or clinical depression is more serious. When you reach the point where you feel incapable of coping with the demands of every-day life, clinical depression may have set in. Depression of this degree is serious and may require professional intervention. Do not wait to seek professional help.[2]

It is extremely painful to realize that we will never again be with our child in this life. Yet we know that we don't own our children, for God has loaned them to us in trust, and He may transfer a young one to His home at any time. We can't bring a child back again, but we can go to be with him or her (See 2 Samuel 12:23).

SHARE YOUR THOUGHTS WITH FAMILY AND FRIENDS

One way to deal with depression is to share your feelings with family and friends. Talking to someone will help you cope with the emotional pain and work through your grief. This may take many months of introspection, self-examination, and discussion. Holding your feelings in can contribute to depression. In addition to family and friends, a pastor or mental health professional can also make a good listener.

It should be remembered, however, that communication between be-reaved fathers and mothers can be problematic at times. Sanders em-phasizes that understanding the grief of a spouse is never an easy task, "because men and women have been socialized to fill different roles. A man is socialized to be unemotional, self-sufficient, and in control. A woman, on the other hand is socialized to be nurturing and empathet-ic, the family communicator."[3]

Rando notes that a dad will generally focus on "controlling his feelings, when what he needs to do is to identify and express them."[4] On the other hand, mothers are prone to express their emotions and to accept help from others but have more difficulty expressing anger.

To avoid family conflict, it is important that moms and dads allow for differences in grief style. Every person grieves differently, so it would be unwise for you to try to force a change in your partner's style. But you can give your husband or wife the permission to open up in expressions of grief if he or she so wishes. For instance, if you are the husband, you can let your wife know that it is alright for her to show anger, and if you are the wife, you can let your husband know it is okay for him to express his feelings verbally or in tears.

In cases where bereaved fathers and mothers are greatly out of synch with each other, support should be sought from sources other than the spouse. Comfort lies in seeking solace from neutral sources among other family and friends, leaving the spouse at peace and removing pressure from the marriage. It should be emphasized that different styles of mourning are to be expected and that there is no right or wrong way to grieve.

As you and your spouse continue to work on your grief, remember that it is very important that you strive to maintain hope during the process. As time goes on, the pain of grief will dissipate and life will eventually have meaning for you again. Let me assure you that these are not hopes that would invalidate your current intense grief, but realistic aspirations that are needed as you respond to the death of your beloved child.

EAT WELL, EXERCISE, AND GET ADEQUATE SLEEP

The depression resulting from the loss of a child can bring about physical reactions. Our minds and our bodies function together, so stress in one area can cause stress in another. Bereavement can affect our physical health.[5]

Some of the physical symptoms that are common in grief are decreased energy, decreased or increased sexual desire, dizziness, empty feelings, gastrointestinal disturbances, heart palpations, lack of appetite, lethargy, irritability, nervousness, physical exhaustion, restlessness, shortness of breath, sleep difficulties (too much or too little), tearfulness, trembling, sighing, and weight loss or gain, among others.

During this period, increased stress can adversely affect your ability to sleep. You may have trouble falling asleep, be troubled by disturbing dreams, awake often in the night and not be able to go back to sleep, or awake early in the morning exhausted.

Some people lose their appetites and fail to eat healthy food. Others eat more as a way of coping with stress. Because of physical exhaustion or apathy, a grief-stricken parent may also neglect physical exercise. It is very important that you work to maintain your health through a well-balanced diet, physical exercise, and proper sleep.

Strive to eat balanced meals in proper portions. Remember also to eat even at times when you are not hungry, but not to overeat if you are prone to using food for comfort. In addition, don't forget to drink lots of water. Grief can sometimes override the thirst mechanism and lead to dehydration.

Exercise regularly. Jog, walk, bicycle, or do aerobics in a systematic manner. Regular exercise promotes physical health as well as mental health. It helps relieve stress, anxiety, depression, and feelings of aggression. Outdoor exercise in the fresh air can be especially uplifting.

Feelings of exhaustion and fatigue are common in grief. If you feel tired during the day, lie down for short rest periods or take an afternoon nap. Try to develop a relaxing bedtime routine so you're ready for sleep at night. Take the phone off the hook, shower or bathe, listen to quiet music, sip a tasteful beverage, and unwind from the stress of the day. Bedtime is also a good time to read your Bible and pray. Expressing your thoughts in prayer and handing your burdens to the Lord can have a soothing, calming effect on you before sleep.

EMBRACE A POSITIVE COPING STYLE

During the major life transition caused by the loss of a child, you will make choices about how you will respond. O'Connor points out that there are four possible responses to change: "(1) Conservation, which involves attempting to remain in the present or to return to the past; (2) Revolution, or aggressively rejecting the past, denying the present, and damning the future; (3) Escape, or evading the present anguish and pain; and (4) Transcendence, or going beyond grief and loss to reorganize your life."[6]

Attempting to shut out the anguish of present suffering by mentally remaining in the refuge of the past is a feature of the conservation style. It is a way of living life as if nothing has changed. A parent who sets up a permanent shrine to a deceased child and who continues to live as though the child has not died is an example.

The revolution style of coping is a way of denying the present pain by rejecting former values, beliefs, and lifestyle. For instance, a parent who decides to join a motorcycle gang and who rebels and fights against everything that formerly provided stability in life is using the revolution style.

Escape is a negative style of coping in which a parent abuses alcohol, drugs or other addictive substances, or tries to escape through behaviors such as gambling and promiscuity. An individual who uses the escape method is refusing to think on the past or to analyze feelings of the present to come to terms with grief or with life.

The transcendent method is a positive coping style which utilizes honesty with self, openness to self-examination, reflection on feelings, and flexibility to change. Don't miss out on the resolution of your grief by refusing to deal with it in a positive manner.

SEEK OUT INFORMATION ON THE GRIEVING PROCESS

It has been said that knowledge is power. Mourning moms and dads desperately need instructions on what to expect, what is normal, and how to confront the dilemmas they face. Many grieving parents report the experience of being pulled into a violent eddy — feeling that they are spinning out of control. Confusion compounds the situation. They feel themselves swirling in turbulent, uncharted waters without a guide or chart to tell them how to cope or mourn.

Bernstein writes that "mourners desperately need to find order and predictability. Books and groups of other bereaved parents provide an anchor. It is reassuring to see that others are indeed experiencing the same violent, chaotic emotions."[7]

Many good books on grief and mourning can be found at local and school libraries and bookstores. Bereaved parents who want to search for additional assistance in dealing with grief can find more help at their library in the form of internet resources on the subject. Capable librarians are available to give assistance in the search.

For many parents, participation in a support group, which serves as a frame of reference by providing models, ideas, and suggestions about how others have dealt with grief, can be most helpful. By joining a self-help group, you will come into contact with other parents going through experiences similar to yours. Members give support as they share information, provide encouragement, and give practical advice for managing grief. As you listen to their stories, you will take comfort in knowing that you are not alone in your grief. Bereaved Parents of the USA and Compassionate Friends are two excellent examples.

The internet has numerous informative resources for mourners, including articles about grief, internet chat groups set up for bereaved parents, and sites devoted to organizations that help grievers. For additional information on grief organizations, including some Web sites, refer to the "Web Site Resources" at the end of the book.

Read books on grief or get help through support groups, but as you do, don't forget the greatest book of all, God's Book! In Psalm 119:105, the Word of God is referred to as "a lamp to my feet and a light to my path." You can count on the Bible to light your way through the darkness. The Good Book provides hope, comfort, guidance, assurance, peace, and so much more! Dwell on the words of the Living God.

OBTAIN PROFESSIONAL HELP IF YOU NEED IT

Emotions can control our lives if we fail to make progress in the work of processing our grief. The death of a child ranks as the most significant death loss that anyone can ever experience. Sanders reports that a child's death "takes much longer to process, because the factors involved are compounded."[8] She notes that some of the compounding factors faced by parents are: resolving guilt and anger; relinquishing the parent-child bond; and grieving not only for the loss of their child, but also for lost aspects of themselves.

The grief after the loss of a child is one of the hardest and longest types of loss to face, yet we know that it is in experiencing our grief and in coming to terms with our own feelings that we can actively move through the phases of grief toward healing and restoration. As you endeavor to work through your grief, it is important for you to monitor your emotions to see if you are making progress and to seek professional help if needed.

Sanders points out that there are some indicators that can signal that a parent probably needs additional help in dealing with bereavement.[9] They include: (1) avoiding friends and relatives rather than honestly communicating with them; (2) failing to eat properly, get enough sleep, or tend to basic self-care needs; (3) denying your loss; (4)having obsessive self-destructive or suicidal thoughts; (5) taking your anger out on people close to you or on yourself; (6) becoming immobilized by grief and unable to see hope for the future; (7) masking your feelings through self-medication, alcohol, or other substance abuse; (8) engaging in foolish acts, such as becoming addicted to gambling or other compulsive behavior; (9) having a history of severe emotional problems; (10) having a feeling that you are falling apart or are no longer in control; (11) having a lack of interest or joy in life even though sufficient time has elapsed; (12) being consistently told by family or friends that they think you need professional assistance; (13) Having your minister or your personal physician refer you to a mental health professional.

Once you decide you are interested in obtaining professional assistance, you will need to find a qualified mental health clinician who fits with you. You can obtain referrals from sources such as friends or relatives, mental health organizations, members of the clergy, your personal physician, support group lists of preferred experts, and so forth. As you look for a therapist, rid yourself of the notion that depression is something to be ashamed of. Treat it as you would any physical pain or illness that invades your life and requires treatment for renewed health.

In your search for a qualified expert, it is important that you find someone who not only has professional training in the mental health field, but who also has understanding in regard to bereavement following the loss of a child. In addition, you should find someone you are personally comfortable with and who you think is helping you to process your grief. Look around until you can find someone with whom you can really connect. Also, bear in mind that counseling and therapy take time because the resolution of grief is difficult and slow work.

SEEK SOLACE FROM GOD

When you lose a child, it is easy to look at the bigness of your circumstances and to feel overwhelmed. You may be questioning, "How did this happen?" "What am I going to do?" " How can I make it through this?"

The more you contemplate your circumstances, the deeper you sink, until finally you feel as if you are going to drown in your grief. But focusing on your circumstance inhibits you from seeing the ability of God to bring you safely through the ordeal.

In your struggle with depression, your victory lies in keeping your eyes clearly focused on the Lord. Remember that God is always bigger than your life circumstances. Even when things look uncertain and your life seems to be falling apart, keep your eyes firmly on him, as you believe to "see the goodness of the Lord" (Psalm 27:13) in your life.

How long shall I take counsel in my soul, having sorrow in my heart all the day?

— Psalm 13:2

4

Surviving Panic

After the death of your child, you may find that you are unable to get your mind off your loss or focus on routine matters. This may cause anxiety and a feeling that you are losing control.

Keep in mind, however, that grief is not just sadness, but a whole host of emotions. This includes difficulty making conversation, disorganized behavior, flashbacks, hyperactivity, inability to make decisions, irritability, loss of interest in personal appearance, preoccupation with events surrounding the death, repetitive dreams, and a sense of meaninglessness. These and other symptoms can rapidly alternate or recur, which in turn can foster a feeling of panic.[1]

In addition, you may be asking questions, such as, "How can I bear this horrible tragedy?" "How will I survive?" "What am I supposed to do to be a good griever?"

You will need to understand that these problems and questions are only temporary conditions that will pass with time. You are simply experiencing a normal part of grief. Other bereaved parents have traveled this same pathway and survived. You will too.

DON'T PANIC IF YOU CAN'T
GET THE LOSS OFF YOUR MIND

As a grieving parent, you may find yourself becoming concerned because you can think of nothing but your loss. You try very hard to get your mind off the subject, but you can't. You probably can agree with the psalmist, who prayed, "How long shall I take counsel in my soul, having sorrow in my heart all the day" (Psalm 13:2). This single-minded focus on your grief seems to be affecting your life in vital areas such as personal relationships, job performance, and social aspects.

For a bereaved parent, interaction in close personal relationships can be hampered because the distraction of grief causes you to be less adept in communicating with others. For example, when people talk to you or ask you questions, you may have to ask them over and over to repeat what was said. Your effectiveness on your job can be affected, too, because you may have problems concentrating, processing information, organizing facts, or making decisions relevant to your work.[2]

Socially, your lack of interest in former values may cause you to want to spend less time with those who place great value on climbing the social ladder or acquiring creature comforts. Because your focus on "things" has diminished, you find materialistic values unacceptable. In addition, you feel a sense of impatience with people who complain about trivial matters, discuss inconsequential subjects, or engage in petty gossip.[3]

It is important for you to realize that preoccupation with grief is a reflection of the internal grief work being done as you sift through every aspect of the death. This single-mindedness excludes other concerns, for you are deeply preoccupied with the internal reality of the severed relationship, with your understanding of it, and with managing your reaction. This is basically why nothing else matters as much to you at this time.

An essential component of the grief process for parents is the search for the cause and meaning of their child's death. In this regard, bereaved moms and dads can expect to deal with death related questions for a long time, such as: "How did it happen?" "Why did it happen?" "How could it have been prevented?" "What occurred just before the death?" Our minds grow weary as we ask such questions over and over.

Yet we feel a need to understand or comprehend as best we can by piecing together a "story" that will give us some answers to our questions. Brook Noel writes that "we need to fact-find and uncover a beginning, middle, and end [to our story] so that we can quit the relentless questioning that keeps us from moving forward."[4] She adds that it is important for us to find answers so that we won't spend more time than necessary recycling the past, and can begin to deal with the present and future.

Although some questions about a child's death can be answered, other questions regarding why it happened or how it fits into the scheme of life can be difficult to answer. For example, a parent whose child is a victim of suicide may never know why the child chose to end his or her own life. It is unwise for such a parent to torture him or herself with questions on a subject for which there may be incomplete or unknown answers. Rather, the parent may need to just "let it go" and move on.

Even when we don't understand or have all the answers, it is good to know that we have a God whose "understanding is infinite" (See Psalm 147:5), Who understands all the "hows," "whats," and "whys," and upon Whom we can depend to take care of our lives.

DON'T WORRY IF YOU ARE UNABLE TO FOCUS ON TASKS

As a grieving parent, you may be wondering why you are having difficulty focusing on even the simplest of tasks. Although concentration is difficult after most losses, when a child dies, parents may find it impossible to focus on routine matters. A jumble of thoughts continually bombards our minds as we struggle desperately to absorb the shock of the horrible tragedy that has befallen us. Even usual distractions, like watching television or light reading, no longer offer an escape, because our minds simply cannot quit racing long enough to allow us to focus.

In fact, as Sanders observes, even "our habitual tasks now require forethought. Before the death, there were things we usually did without thinking, like making the bed, straightening the kitchen, or cooking. But after such a loss, simply preparing breakfast can be an impossible task."[5] Until parents have had the chance to integrate the loss of a child into their lives, they usually experience a long period of confusion and loss of concentration. As they try to get control of chaotic emotions, they experience a continuing inability to readily focus on daily activities that need to be done.

Your grief may also cause you to be highly distracted, disoriented, and befuddled. For instance, on occasion you may find yourself arriving at a destination and not recalling how you got there, stopping at green lights rather than red, or receiving a traffic ticket because you were speeding but didn't realize you were. Situations such as this can be dangerous, both to you and others, so due diligence is required. Letting someone else drive or taking public transportation is a safer alternative.

In addition, grief will cause you to have problems in thinking through decisions or making choices. For this reason, it is advisable for you to refrain from making major decisions relating to such things as job, housing, or relationship changes soon after your loss. You may have to temporarily rely on other trusted sources of support for objective feedback on problems and decisions. In minor areas where memory lapses or lack of concentration cause problems, you can give yourself support by using lists and agendas to keep your thinking straight.

Problems such as the foregoing may heighten your anxiety or cause you to feel panicky that you may be losing control. However, you will need to recognize that these problems in thinking and decision making are only temporary conditions that will pass with grief work and the passage of time. They are a natural and normal aspect of your grief.

BE PATIENT WITH YOURSELF AS YOU GRIEVE

As time goes on and the severity of your grief does not seem to dissipate as quickly as you would wish, you may begin to panic that you will never "get over" your grief. It is important to remember that you can't chart out a course or determine a time frame for grief.[6] The fact is that in a sense you will never actually "get over it." The relationship that was yours with your son or daughter will never be there again in this life. So, in some ways, you will always be "in the process."

People often quote the maxim that time heals all wounds, meaning that if we just wait long enough, the pain of grief will go away. The pain never goes completely away, but it will lessen. The therapeutic aspect of time is that it can allow you to put things in perspective, process feelings, adapt to change, and attend to grief work. These experiences, plus the passage of time, reduce your pain. But the passage of time can only help you adapt if you are actively engaged in your grief work.

Many people also incorrectly assume that as grief diminishes with time, it goes from high to low in a straight line, and once it declines it never erupts again. Actually, the intensity of your grief will fluctuate over time and have many ups and downs. Some of these fluctuations are caused by events such as anniversaries, holidays, and changes in factors relating to your grief such as diminishing social support or the presence of other stresses in life. When this happens, you may find it frustrating to have to feel your grief anew after experiencing a break.

Grief takes much time and energy and will progress at an uneven pace. Some segments of your mourning may be done at one period and other aspects may be stored away to be dealt with later. You will alternate between making progress and backsliding, but you will never go as far back as you were in the beginning. Be patient and do not place unrealistic expectations on yourself or other family members in regard to a time frame for healing.

DON'T ALLOW OTHERS TO PUSH YOU THROUGH GRIEF

Some friends may expect you to return to your "old self" or to "get better" before you have had time to grieve. Bernstein points out that many times they think there is a schedule to follow in grief: "Self-appointed experts, professionals, clergy, and well-meaning friends and family are ready with solace, exhortations, and ultimately the admonition that it's time to 'get on with your life,' as if life could ever be the same."[7]

When you're in the throes of grief, it's easy to feel like you're doing it all wrong. Friends and professionals can compound the uncertainty when they suggest you should be conducting your grief according to their time frame. Don't allow friends, or anyone else, to push you through the mourning process or to set a time frame for you. Recognize that your grief will be unique to you and to your own loss. It will be shaped by your personal characteristics and by the unique group of factors that describe your particular loss.

Remember, too, that it doesn't make any difference what others think. It's your loss and your grief. We each have to grieve at our own pace, even if that pace is different from what our friends would expect or like. It is true, however, that the course of mourning can proceed more quickly for some than for others. Some grieving parents find purpose and meaning quite quickly, while other parents remain in the deepest shadows much longer. Most of the time, however, the journey through grief is difficult work and takes a lot of time, determination, and persistent effort.

Oftentimes, a bereaved parent is forced to don a mask of social propriety by putting on a happy face. Indeed, many bereaved parents put on their happy mask not only with friends, extended family, and work associates, but also, at times, even with a spouse. For many deeply grieving moms and dads, the only times they can take off their masks are when they are alone or with a truly understanding, sympathetic person such as another bereaved parent.

You'll never have to worry about donning a mask for the Lord, because He already knows everything about you, so you can be open and honest with Him. God knows every detail of your life, "indeed, the very hairs of your head are numbered" (Luke 12:7), and He places utmost value and worth upon you. God knows, and He cares.

*Come to me, all who
are weary and heavy-laden,
and I will give you rest.*

— Matthew 11:28

5

Surviving Guilt

The "natural" order of life, we are taught, is that children die after their parents, not before them. When a child goes first, it is not unusual for parents to feel overwhelmed by a sense of guilt and regret.

DON'T ASSUME RESPONSIBILITY
FOR THINGS YOU CANNOT CONTROL

Keep in mind that as a parent, you are experiencing one of the most dreaded events that can occur in life, so it is normal for you to feel guilt. Guilt is a natural by-product of grief no matter what the loss, but the guilt of a parent is doubly pronounced. When something happens to our children, we immediately blame ourselves because we feel responsible for them. We reason that if we had been more on guard, the death would never have occurred.

We live in a society that expects parents to be totally responsible for their children's care. If something happens to our child, we feel that we are at fault, that we should have been taking better care to prevent harm. "If only" are two words uttered over and over again as we blame ourselves for what happened. Instead of moving forward, we scroll backward to recant the "if onlys" of a past we cannot change. As we continue the self-blame game, we halt the grieving process. Guilt is completely unproductive and will only delay recovery and healing.[1]

You may be in the process of searching your soul to discover what it is that you did or did not do that could have prevented your child's death.

These thoughts and feelings are common, but know that in time they will pass. In the meantime, focus on being gentle and kind to yourself.

When guilt and condemnation overwhelm you, recognize the fact that God does not want you to condemn yourself for things you cannot control.

MAKE A DISTINCTION
REAL & UNJUSTIFIED GUILT

There are basically two types of guilt in grief. Guilt that is out of proportion to the event is called unjustified or illegitimate guilt. On the other hand, when there is a direct cause-and-effect relationship between something you did or failed to do that caused harm to the deceased, that type of guilt is considered real or legitimate guilt.[2]

Unjustified guilt is the normal consequence of the parent/child relationship which is, by its nature, flawed. Keep in mind that parents are human beings and, as such, make mistakes and have ambivalent feelings in relationships. Unjustified guilt often comes from overly high standards you may have placed upon yourself.

For example, after your child's death, you may have said something such as: "I should have been able to prevent my child's death." Or, "During our relationship, I never should have felt anger toward my youngster." Comments such as these reveal you have been holding unrealistic expectations for yourself. In many cases, even if you have been an exemplary parent, you will still focus on something you think you did wrong or did not do at all.

To determine if you are experiencing unjustified guilt, you may want to discuss your feelings with a trusted and nonjudgmental person, either professional or nonprofessional, who can help you examine events rationally to decide if you did act in the best way possible under the circumstance. If you are indeed experiencing false guilt, don't continue to harbor guilt or regret that you didn't do or say more.

Who can find a time when we were perfect? When our child dies, there is always something more we could have done; there is always something more we could have said; there is always something more. Cast aside unjustified guilt or regrets, both those thrust upon you and those of your own making.

Legitimate or real guilt occurs when your guilt is appropriate to the event, when there is a direct cause-and-effect role between something you did or did not do and harm which resulted to your deceased child. This may have been a purposeful action or inaction which caused harm. Or, it may have been an unintentional action or lack of action that produced hurt to your child.

An example of a purposeful act is the highly publicized case in which a suicidal mother intentionally drove a car, with her little children inside, into a lake. The mom changed her mind about suicide and saved herself by jumping out of the car, but left her small children inside to drown.

An instance of an unintentional act might occur when parents in charge of watching out for a child fail to perform that responsibility through inattention or oversight. An example of inattention could be the case of a parent who dozes off poolside while supervising a child, resulting in the drowning death of the youngster. An example of oversight might be when a mother and a father both presume the other parent is supervising a child, but each fails to communicate that fact to the other person, and as a consequence the child dies. A case in point would be a child left sleeping in a car in hot weather, because each parent thought the other had taken the child from the vehicle.

In cases where failure of a parent to protect a child is not purposeful, the father or mother responsible will nevertheless probably suffer from a tremendous sense of guilt and blame. If you are a parent who is experiencing guilt because of an unintentional act or inaction, you may need to seek professional psychiatric assistance in order to deal with your sense of guilt. It is vitally important that you come to terms with the fact that what happened was an accident so you can forgive yourself.

DON'T BLAME YOURSELF FOR YOUR CHILD'S SUICIDE

For parents, the suicide of a child is one of the most difficult deaths with which to cope. Such a death burdens the mourning parent with extra guilt and prolongs the healing process. Intense guilt is quite common because when a child takes his or her own life, parents tend to think they could have prevented it. Parental self-reproach is also prominent because fathers and mothers often blame themselves for not recognizing the depth of their child's despair and for not taking action. Typically they ask themselves over and over how they failed as parents.[3]

If your child has been a victim of his or her own suicidal actions, no doubt you will mentally pore over and over the events of the days and weeks preceding the death searching for answers and trying to make sense of this senseless event. You will also ask questions that can never be answered because the only person who can verify the answers is dead. You will ask, "Why did my child do this?" "Why didn't my youngster tell me things were so bad?" "Why couldn't I stop my offspring from doing this?" "What did I do wrong?"

These and numerous other questions will consume you if you let them. You can spend years going over detail after detail preceding the event and punish yourself needlessly for what you think you should have said or done that might have made a difference. But actually, guilt of this nature accomplishes nothing except to make you feel worse and to prolong your emotional misery.

Don't let guilt hold you hostage. Suicidal death can have incredible power over the lives of surviving parents and other family members, leaving them with confusion and guilt over the death. Whatever happened in the past, keep in mind that you did the best you could at the time. You need to forgive yourself so you can begin to move on with the rest of your life. Don't allow past memories to retain the power to ruin your present life.

The following are some suggestions for parents who have lost a child to suicide: focus on what you were able to do for your child, not on what you didn't do; talk to friends or family; seek out support groups for survivors of suicide; talk to a professional counselor trained in working with families of suicides; learn to forgive yourself and move on with your life.

Remember, you do not have to bear the heavy burden of your child's death alone. In Matthew 11:28, the Lord promises rest for those who come to Him: "Come to me, all who are weary and heavy laden, and I will give you rest." Allow Him to carry your load.

TALK TO A PROFESSIONAL ABOUT YOUR FEELINGS OF GUILT

Following the death of a child, bereaved parents often struggle with a host of guilt feelings. For instance, if a youngster died from disease or illness, surviving parents may have lingering doubts about decisions made regarding treatment, such as whether they might have missed early symptoms, whether they allowed the child to go through too much treatment, and so forth. Past decisions in regard to care of the child are questioned endlessly, even though parents may have actually done the very best that they could in caring for their child.

Mourning parents may also feel guilt concerning our inability to save our children. No matter what we did, we were unable to make things better. Consequently, we feel inadequate and guilty that we could not prevent the death. Survivor guilt may occur too. The meaning of life is questioned, because we wonder why we should be allowed to go on living, when our child has been deprived of a future here on earth.

Guilt about ambivalent feelings is likewise common. It is perfectly normal that conflicting feelings should exist, yet we feel guilty that while our child was still alive we may have experienced anger or resentment directed toward the young person. No relationship is perfect. All relationships are mixtures of positive and negative emotions. Yet, following our youngster's death, we may dwell on memories of negative emotions until they become gigantic in our minds, and we torture ourselves with guilt for having conflicting feelings toward a son or daughter.

Another source of guilt is perceived misdeeds. A parent may have failed in some aspect of life, and now he or she sees the child's death as punishment for mistakes or misdeeds. For instance, an alcoholic parent may interpret the loss of a child as punishment for the parent's excessive drinking. In addition, moms or dads may experience guilt about public reactions to the death. Despite the fact that we are fighting a heroic battle just to survive our pain, we perceive that perhaps we have failed to act in a way that society expects of us. We may think we over-reacted or under-reacted at the funeral, so we feel guilty for not acting the "right" way. What we fail to remember is that there really is no right or wrong way to grieve.

The most common types of guilt bereaved parents suffer have been examined here, but there are many other forms. It will be helpful to the progress of your grief work if you talk about whatever kind of guilt reactions you are experiencing with someone you trust. Sanders elaborates that guilt held inside becomes destructive, but the "way to exorcise guilt is to share guilty feelings with supportive, caring people."[4]

Talk about your guilt feelings with someone you trust, or if you feel ready for group situations, seek out self-help groups. Chances are, others have experienced the same feelings too. In addition, don't be afraid or embarrassed to talk about your feelings of guilt with a professional qualified to counsel you on parental grief. An expert counselor can give you valuable insight and advice on how to conquer feelings of guilt.

In order to let go of guilt, you will need to constantly remind yourself that under the circumstances you did the best you could. Refuse to dwell on negative feelings of guilt, but turn your thinking instead toward positive thoughts and your trust in the Lord.

RECOGNIZE GOD'S SOVEREIGN CONTROL OF LIFE

Guilt and regret are part of the human condition, but there can be no guilt for events beyond our control. The Lord doesn't want us to feel guilty about something that ultimately was out of our hands. The time of our passing is determined by God's sovereign control. As Psalm 31:15 informs us, our "times are in Thy hand."

It will help us to overcome guilty feelings when we can acknowledge the fact that God has everything under control and that things happen for a reason, even if we can't understand the reason now. When we try to figure things out for ourselves, we attempt to take the reins into our own hands and push God aside. But when we trust in God, we don't have to understand "why" to be able to face the future without guilt or condemnation. The revelation of God's sovereignty can pull us out of the guilt.

Let God be God beyond your understanding. It is only when our hearts no longer demand answers that God can and will redeem the pain for our good and for His glory. When we can place the sovereignty of God beside His unfailing love, then our hearts can rest.

Be angry, and yet do not sin; do not let the sun go down on your anger.

— Ephesians 4:26

6

Surviving Anger

Anger is another emotion to be expected to some degree after the death of a child. The anger need not be overly intense or necessarily be displayed through screaming infuriation, but may be seen in milder variations such as irritability, intolerance, frustration, or annoyance. The resentment we feel is a natural consequence of our being deprived of something greatly valued by us, our child.[1]

Mankind is not alone in the experience of anger. Anger is an emotion felt by God when He is provoked by the disobedience, error, or sin of human beings. The same emotions are shared by God and mankind because God created man in His own image (See Genesis 1:27).

Feelings of anger are normal for grieving parents, although we may endeavor to sublimate these feelings. If feelings of anger do exist, it would be extremely harmful to us if we could not admit to ourselves that we are indeed very irate about one or more aspects of our loss and take actions to dispel that anger.

LET FRIENDS AND PROFESSIONALS HELP YOU COPE WITH YOUR ANGER

Anger in the bereaved parent comes from many things. There is anger about being deprived of a future with our child and anger about our feelings of frustration and helplessness. Anger can even be directed at society in general, at the world at large, at organized religion, or at any other source.

You have a right to feel your emotions. Anger is a part of your grief, a real and normal reaction to your feelings of loss, deprivation, confusion, and despair. Keep in mind, however, that resentment carried for too long can be destructive. Harry and Cheryl Salem point out that "anger is an honest emotion. We may feel angry for a few days, weeks, or even months, but eventually, those feelings must be dealt with. Unchecked anger doesn't fix anything. It doesn't do anyone any good, and it only brings harm to the person who is angry."[2]

It is important that you quickly deal with your anger by talking with a trusted friend or professional who can accept your rage and listen as you recount your bitter feelings. Don't hide or be ashamed of your feelings. Hiding your anger won't make it go away. You'll work it out of your system more quickly if you can bring it out into the open.

Remember too that Scripture declares that anger left unresolved over a long period can lead to sin, as noted in Ephesians 4:26, where we are told: "Be angry, and yet do not sin; do not let the sun go down on your anger." This passage reminds us that we can be angry for a time, but we are to resolve our angry feelings quickly.

Don't Blame Innocent Others for Your Loss

Anger may be turned inward and be experienced as depression, or it may be projected outward onto other people.[3] When we project anger onto others, often we do so because we need someone to blame for what has happened to our child. Often feelings of anger and hostility are directed toward those who are closest to us, our family members. Parents are especially prone to blame each other for the loss of a child. At times, parental anger is displaced onto other individuals such as ambulance drivers, hospital workers, and so forth.

Of course, justified anger can stem from cases of homicide, suicide, or self-destructive behavior. For instance, if your child has been murdered, one would expect you to be enraged that someone would kill your beloved child. If your child took his or her own life, you also would be expected to be angry at the child for ending a young life and imposing tremendous heartache upon you. Anger such as this is not easily addressed or resolved.

To confront your anger, you will need to identify your feelings, admit your anger to yourself, and then communicate it to someone you trust.[4] A good friend, a professional counselor, or a pastor can help you to address your feelings of anger or rage. Another way to deal with pent-up emotions is to release them through physical activity such as walking, running, swimming, or working out. While physical activity is helpful, it is only a temporary solution to let off steam. It will be wise for you to plan a longer-term program such as counseling or group support, to assist you in getting into contact with your anger and resolving it.

LET A CHILD WHO DIES BY
SUICIDE ACCEPT RESPONSIBILITY

When a child dies by suicide, it is logical for the parents to feel some anger toward the youngster. Drug abuse or other self-destructive actions resulting in a child's death might also contribute to angry feelings directed toward the child. When a child's death is a result of risky behavior, as Sanders points out, the parents "are usually, and quite naturally, angry at the deceased child."[5]

There can be anger that the child purposely chose to leave you, anger that the child's death has thrown your life into turmoil, anger that you have been deprived of the child's companionship, and anger that the suicide deprived the child of a future. It is very sad for you to realize that you will never get to see a son or daughter grow to adulthood, possibly marry and bear children, all because of a willful act of self-destruction.

Recognize that you are particularly victimized by a death resulting from either suicide or self-destructive behavior and susceptible to intensified bereavement reactions. Your anger may be directed toward your deceased child, toward yourself, or toward other people. If your anger is directed toward your child, you may be uncomfortable with your anger at the one now dead. Realize, however, that your anger is normal and that you will need to confront it, not deny it.

If you are angry toward yourself, you may be assuming that you could have done something to prevent the death. For example, in regard to a suicidal death, do not place unrealistic blame or anger on yourself for missing or not responding to possible hints or clues about an impending act that now makes sense to you in the light of hindsight. You will need to recognize the limits of your ability to have prevented a suicide, for none of us is ultimately responsible for or in control of another person's choices, even if that person is a child.

The same advice goes if you are angry toward other people for not preventing a child's self-destructive act. For instance, you might feel anger toward someone to whom your child confided suicidal thoughts, because the person did not take action to prevent the death. Again, remember that hindsight is 20/20. The suicidal intentions of a child may not be recognized or taken seriously at the time by another person.

Consignment for the actions of your youngster cannot be assumed by you or by anyone else. In the final analysis, we are accountable only for our own choices, whether good or bad. Don't accept responsibility yourself or place fault on others for the purposeful self-destructive actions of your child.

The past is gone now, so let it go. You can trust in God's love, both for your child and for yourself, and look toward the future with comfort and hope in your heart.

YOU MAY FEEL ANGER TOWARD GOD

You may be angry with God for what you feel is the injustice and unfairness of your child's death. Your realization that something is wrong and awareness that you can't make sense of it may lead you to experience anger toward Him. You may ask questions, such as: If God is all powerful, why did He allow this loss? Doesn't God realize how much my child's death has hurt me? If God loves me, why doesn't He do something? Where is God? These and similar questions evoke anger.

Is anger at God wrong or dangerous? When we are angry at God, what are we to do? God is not threatened by our anger, but wants us to grow beyond it. If you are angry at God, it is better for you to acknowledge rather than hide your feelings. Talk to Him about your anger and about how you feel.

Consider your relationship with God as similar to that of any other relationship. If you were angry at a person, but retreated into a shell rather than voicing your feelings toward the individual, a wall would form between you. Likewise, you build up a wall if you do not communicate your deep thoughts to God. As with any other relationship, it is better to acknowledge your feelings and tear down the wall, than to hide your feelings and risk becoming bitter.

A mistaken view of God may cause us to feel abandoned by the Lord. If we believe that our Creator will only allow good things to happen to us, it is implied that God has abandoned us when difficult times come. It should be noted, however, that nowhere in Scripture does God promise us freedom from suffering. What He does promise is comfort and help, for He has not "abhorred the affliction of the afflicted, neither has He hidden His face from him; but when he cried to Him for help, He heard" (Psalm 22:24).

FORGIVE OTHERS AND YOURSELF

Forgiveness can be one of the most difficult aspects to achieve in the process of working through grief. Sometimes we are unable to move forward because we need to first release our angry emotions before we can get to the place where we can actually forgive. To achieve a forgiving spirit, you must face the reality of what took place when your child died and why you are angry at someone, whether that person is yourself, another person, or even your deceased child. Then you must process your angry emotions by choosing to give up resentments and by releasing the energy that has kept you in bondage.

But what exactly is forgiveness? Noel provides an excellent definition: "Forgiveness simply means that we acknowledge the deep pain we feel, but choose to move past that pain. We forgive those who contributed to our pain and let their actions become part of our past."[6] She adds that forgiveness doesn't mean we are condoning hurtful actions or forgetting how much we hurt. Rather, we are able to forgive someone despite the fact that we dislike what he or she has done.

Remember that if your anger is directed toward your deceased child because the young person took his or her own life by carelessness or by design, you must find a way to release the anger you are feeling. Or, if there was a traumatic relationship between you two while he or she was still alive, you must let go of that, too. When we lose a loved one during a rocky point in our relationship, such as during the rebellious teen years, we may recall hurtful words that were exchanged. While conflicts cannot be resolved directly with the child anymore, we can still resolve them in our hearts by letting go of anger and by practicing forgiveness.

Even when we are able to forgive others, however, we often find it difficult to forgive ourselves because we may hold ourselves to an unrealistic standard we wouldn't expect from someone else. By amplifying our own mistakes, and by holding ourselves hostage to our own perceived misdeeds, we neglect to forgive ourselves and thereby prevent forward progress in our lives.

If left unresolved, anger can be harmful because it can steal your peace, make your heart bitter, destroy your relationships, and keep you from healing and moving forward. Yet by the grace of God, unsettled anger can be overcome. One of the most important lessons we can learn from grief is that we don't have to suffer long years of pain because of unresolved feelings of anger toward others or even toward ourselves. We can release resentful feelings by replacing the negative feelings and bitterness at the root of our anger with the positive feelings of joy, peace, and contentment. In this way, as we rely upon God's grace and power in our lives, we can truly achieve victory over anger.

And He said to them,
"Come away by yourselves to
a lonely place and
rest a while."

— Mark 6:31

7

Surviving Physical Aspects of Grief

As already mentioned, grief not only affects you emotionally, it can also affect your physical health. Doctors have connected enduring stress to a breakdown of the immune system, which consequently invites forms of illness. According to Sanders, the ongoing stress of grief can cause changes in "blood pressure, heart rate, and the chemical makeup of blood. Prolonged grief can actually suppress our immune system, leaving us exposed to a variety of illnesses, infections, and maladies."[1]

CONTROL YOUR STRESS

Stress overload is caused by the tremendous trauma and prolonged stress we endure in bereavement.[2] Grief uses an enormous expenditure of mental energy which results in debilitating stress. For parents in mourning, the struggle just to survive each day can sap their strength and leave them vulnerable to illnesses such as viruses, sinusitis, or the flu. In addition major illnesses can result, especially sicknesses that are stress related, such as digestive tract disorders like ulcers, gastritis, or colitis. Blood pressure may also increase significantly during this period, leading to strokes or heart disease.

The continued stress of grief can keep our bodies from returning back to a normal state of balance and health. Resources we normally use to cope with disease may thus be depleted, resulting in possible illness.

This is why it is so important for you to realize that grief can escalate into a serious health risk. You must endeavor to take care of yourself and monitor your health.

Remember also to look to God for help during this time when your emotional and physical resources are drained. You can turn to Him in prayer for comfort, strength, and endurance during this extremely difficult and low point in your life.

DON'T PUSH YOURSELF BEYOND THE LIMITS OF YOUR PHYSICAL ENDURANCE

In an endeavor to cope with the loss of a child, some parents immerse themselves in a flurry of outside activities, work, or other pursuits.[3] Often there can be a "driven" quality to this busy activity, an obsession with throwing themselves into some pursuit, so they won't have time to think about their pain. They may push themselves for hours in non-stop activities that lead to mistreatment of their bodies.

Staying busy is a way to avoid the grieving process by keeping your mind occupied on other information in an attempt to prevent contemplation of your real emotional state. It can also be an attempt to make the internal suffering disappear, a coping mechanism which, unfortunately, doesn't work.

The process of readjustment in the grieving process is a progressive series of measures or changes that get you from one place to another psychologically. Because grieving is a process, you will progress naturally if you just go forward in your grief work. On the other hand, if you resist the mourning process, you are in danger of breaking down physically, mentally, or both. If you have been distracting yourself from grief, realize that you will need to slow down to give yourself the chance to complete your grief work.

Understand too that if you have been diverting yourself with busyness, you may have been sidetracking yourself as well from fellowship with

God, your best ally and true friend. As you begin to slow down and to face the pain you have sought to avoid, you will also provide yourself with an opportunity to renew your fellowship with Him.

PROCESS YOUR GRIEF

Parental grief over the loss of a child not only causes extreme sadness and hurt, it can also load us down with a host of conflicting emotions such as anger, guilt, and fear. You have a choice in regard to how you will handle your various feelings and emotions. One choice is to allow yourself to feel your pain, to process your emotions, and to eventually heal. The other choice is to avoid your grief, to repress your feelings, and to postpone healing.

Grieving is the normal response to the pain and anguish of loss, but if it is repressed, denied, or internalized, it can lead to serious diseases of the body or distress of the emotions.[4] Guilty, hurtful, or angry feelings that we try to repress stay with us for years. By denying them, we merely delay and stretch out the bereavement process. It is much better to quickly deal with our painful memories and to free ourselves from negative emotions. It takes a lot of energy to feel emotions like guilt, rage, or frustration, but it takes more energy in the long run to hold back these emotions.

Repressing grief may actually result in psychosomatic illness, sickness resulting from the interaction between mind and body. There can be a strong correlation between illness and the way in which a great loss is handled. Physical symptoms like headaches, backaches, and other forms of physical distress can be caused by unresolved feelings of guilt, anger, and so forth that are intertwined with the grief.

In cases where repressed grief is a causal factor in illness, more than just the physical symptoms must be addressed. By obtaining psychological as well as medical assistance, a parent can understand the cause of symptoms and eradicate the illness. For psychosomatic illness, healing is accomplished by grief work. By experiencing, expressing, and managing the emotions you feel, you will recover. It may take many months of self-contemplation and professional treatment, but healing will result as you come to emotional terms with your loss.

In coping with the death of your child, you face one of the most agonizing challenges of life. Working through your grief takes energy, time, and perseverance, and you may feel like giving up at times. You have the opportunity, however, once you have processed your grief, to emerge as a stronger, more competent, and more loving person.

Maintain a Healthy
Lifestyle During Grief

To endure the difficult bereavement process and to avoid physical complications, it is essential for you to maintain a healthy lifestyle. Your physical health must be cared for not only to reduce the potential for the development of serious physical problems, but also to preserve your energy for grief work and for the important task of caring for your family.

Your health can be adversely affected if you neglect to have dental and physical check-ups when needed. Excessive tobacco use or high caffeine consumption can add to your problems, too, by making you jittery, keeping you keyed-up, and suppressing your appetite. And, of course, the negative effects alcohol or drug abuse can have on your physical health are well recognized.

Because of their involvement in grief, however, some bereaved parents neglect their health. Caught up in the wounds of their heart and the brokenness of their spirit, they refuse to even bother to think about anything else. Keep in mind, though, that as Cheryl Salem points out, "if we don't look after our own health, we will be no good to anyone else. I have found that I am a better wife, mother, and minister when I do what I need to do to keep my physical body in good working order. The same will be true for you no matter what you're facing in life."[5]

Your loved ones really need you, so take good care of yourself. Remember too that you will need to stay healthy in order to complete the difficult mourning process. God has more for you to do in life, and you must survive to be able to do it. Bear in mind that adequate nutrition, rest, and exercise will benefit your ability to cope with your loss, to meet the demands of your everyday life, and to overcome possible physical illness generated by the stress of your bereavement.

In Scripture, the value of our physical bodies is stressed in Psalms 139:13-14, where our bodies are described as "fearfully and wonderfully made." If God puts such enormous importance and value on our bodies, then we would do well to place high value on them as well.

You May Experience a Second Phase of Need for Extra Rest

After the previous phases of protracted and intense grief have abated somewhat, you may face another period when you need to take time out for added rest. During the earlier stages of grief, our bodies can be flooded with adrenaline, a substance which causes our bodily systems to race. This flooding happens over a prolonged period of time, leaving us feeling extremely depleted and fatigued. You should give in to the fatigue you are now experiencing because it is your body's way of telling you that you need to pull back in order to restore your strength.

It is a positive, adaptive step for you to obey your body, rather than a negative one. So, during the day, take time out for naps when you can, and at night, try to get in at least 8-10 hours of solid sleep. In addition, nurture yourself with some simple pleasures of life such as a bouquet of flowers, a restaurant meal, a soothing massage, or a fragrant bath. You deserve and need to pamper yourself in many ways to help restore your peace and strength.

In this phase, the danger exists that you may fear you are making slow progress and therefore try to accelerate your recovery. But this effort only leads to frustration, for truthfully the pace of grief cannot be hurried. Friends or relatives may also fear for you and try to urge you to be busier. For example, a friend may want you to spend the entire day on a shopping trip when you really don't feel strong enough to do so. If you think a long day traipsing through the mall would overtax your energies, just say no.

Keep in mind that rest and sleep are adaptive responses that will re-energize your body and facilitate your recovery. Do not feel guilty or worried about the fact that you need more sleep than you previously required. In reality you are doing yourself a tremendous favor when you respond to your body's need to repair and regain new balance.

It is comforting to know that Jesus recognized our great need for rest during times of grief. Scripture tells us that when John the Baptist was beheaded by King Herod, the disciples of Jesus heard about the act, took away John's body, and buried it in a tomb. Afterward, they reported their actions to Jesus, who displayed concern for the emotional and physical well-being of His disciples and, in turn, for us, by telling them to "Come away by yourselves to a lonely place and rest awhile" Mark 6:31).

GIVE FAITH A CHANCE TO HELP YOU HEAL

Some research shows that that people with strong religious convictions are better able to recover from illness and enjoy greater overall health. For example, Harold G. Koenig, MD, a Duke University researcher who has spent years studying the link between religion and health and is the author of *The Handbook of Religion and Health*, writes that "there is good science-based research showing an association between religion and good health. These are prospective studies with large samples showing that religion is related to lower blood pressure, greater longevity, and certainly better mental health."[6]

God is called the Great Physician because the power of physical, spiritual, and emotional healing belongs to Him. The Word of God records many instances during the Lord's public ministry when He healed those afflicted with various physical illnesses: "And Jesus was going about in all Galilee ... healing every kind of disease and every kind of sickness among the people" (Matthew 4:23-24). Spiritual healing results, as well, because, for those who fear His name, "the sun of righteousness will rise with healing in its wings" (Malachi 4:2). Good emotional health can also be a by-product of faith, hope, and trust in the dependability of God's provision for our lives, "which is Christ in you, the hope of glory" (Colossians 1:27).

You can turn to God in prayer asking for His healing touch in your life. God's desire is for healing in the totality of your being, so open yourself to the healing work of God and pray that you may be healed.

The Lord your God
is the one who goes with
you. He will not fail
you or forsake you.

— *Deuteronomy 31:6*

8

Surviving Life Changes

After the loss of a son or daughter, grieving parents notice changes in almost every aspect of their lives, including ways they relate to their spouses, to their surviving children, and to their friends.

They also often experience changes within themselves in terms of personal beliefs about life and death, values, priorities, and faith. In addition, they can notice changes associated with key life events such as holidays, birthdays, and anniversaries.

STRIVE TO MAINTAIN A GOOD RELATIONSHIP WITH YOUR SPOUSE

After a child's death, spouses should be supportive, caring, and loving toward one another. But it doesn't always happen that way. Sometimes spouses drift apart. Instead of grieving together, they become privately immersed in their own mourning.

Of course, no one expects them to grieve in the same way. One may want to discuss the pain, while the other does not; one may find comfort in work, while the other feels overwhelmed; one may want to remove memory-triggering articles and photographs from the home, while the other wants them to remain; one may want to protect surviving children from their grief, while the other tries to remain open; one may want to resume sex, while the other is uninterested; one may find comfort in religion, while the other isn't consoled; or one may have difficulty releasing feelings and requesting support, while the other has difficulty expressing anger.[1]

Because of these and numerous other differences in parental grieving, it isn't surprising that studies have shown that marital discord and divorce are common after a child's death. It has been estimated that between 75 to 90 percent of all married couples have serious problems after the loss of a son or daughter.[2] It is vitally important, therefore, that you strive to maintain a good relationship with your spouse. A nonjudgmental attitude is necessary, along with a sustained effort to just be there for each other. Don't worry about trying to communicate verbally or trying to do the "right thing." Easy ways to be supportive and to nurture one another are the simple acts of touching, hugging, and showing signs of kindness and affection.

HELP YOUR SURVIVING CHILDREN COPE WITH THE LOSS OF THEIR SIBLING

Surviving children in a family will greatly suffer from the loss of a sibling and can have a difficult time in discharging their grief.[3] They may, like parents (1) experience survival guilt, (2) feel their parents are abandoning them emotionally, or (3) feel life has lost its innocence or luster. Let's examine each of these conditions.

First, siblings, like parents, sometimes feel they should have been the ones to die — that they are less needed by society than the lost child. Children may also feel responsible for the death, recalling angry emotions they felt toward the child before he or she died and remembering times they said childish things like "I wish you were dead." Then when the brother or sister dies, the surviving child can carry enormous guilt. Thus, it is important that parents check to see if surviving children are experiencing survival guilt and to offer reassurance when needed.

Second, when parents are going through the throes of grief, it can be difficult for them to attend to the emotional needs of their children.

Since they are suffering acute grief themselves, they may lack the patience, emotional resources, or functioning power to be available to their surviving children as in the past. For these reasons, surviving children can feel emotionally abandoned by grieving parents. Despite the severity of your own grief, strive to be there for your offspring, for they need your affection and love now more than ever. Your children will also benefit greatly just from your warm physical presence and your tender explanations or answers to questions.

However, if you feel you cannot meet your children's needs, identify the limitations, and get appropriate help from others. Enlist the aid of a child's teacher, a favorite relative, or a trusted friend to watch the child and to encourage healthy mourning. Even if you can't be a "super parent" at this time, you can still arrange things as much as possible so that your youngster's basic needs can be met. Be honest with your child by letting him or her know that you are having a difficult time too, but that you will get through it together.

Third, it is not uncommon for bereaved siblings to lose a measure of their youthful innocence and joyfulness about life. The death of a brother or sister is a stark and painful reminder that life is fragile. These children may also feel the weight of being a remaining or an only child, with all the implications. Tarnished and wizened at an early age, they are forever robbed of the carefree nature of their childhood.

Children can carry the scars of survival guilt, perceived parental emotional abandonment, and lost innocence for a long time. But this is also an opportunity for a family to come together and strengthen its bonds. Children who receive added support, reassurance, love, and a chance to talk about their feelings will be better able to handle their grief.

Don't Blame Yourself
If Some Friendships Falter

After facing the loss of a child, it is common for parents to see a shift in their circle of friends. Our friendships may change because of personal changes we undergo after a child's death, or because of the stigma attached by others to death and grief, or because of an unrealistic timetable friends may set for our "recovery."

You have just gone through a profound experience, so you may find that your perspective on life has changed, and that your friendship needs have also changed.[4] Many friends and even relatives will not understand the adjustments you have gone through and will wish for the return of your "old self." You have been through a tremendously difficult experience, but these friends may be unable to relate to the new person you have become.

The stigma attached to the subjects of death and grief may also propel a change in friends. Many people today seek happiness and try to avoid any painful or negative feelings. This is why some friends or relatives may be uncomfortable in expressing their condolences. The death of your child and the grief you are experiencing creates pain and sadness for them too. Your loss has brought home to them the fact that death can happen to anyone at any time. Because the grief you are experiencing reminds them of their own family's vulnerability, some of them may avoid contact with you.

Your friends' expectations about when you should recover may also stress your friendships. They may offer directives, such as, "It's been three months, so you should be getting over it by now." Or, "You need to stop thinking about it and move on." On the other hand, friends who say, "You seem to be doing better now," are eager for us to be better. A discreet response might be, "Thanks for your encouraging words, but I know I've just begun."

Keep in mind, however, that the vast majority of your friends and relatives will probably remain steadfast throughout your ordeal. In *A Grace Disguised: How the Soul Grows Through Loss*, Gerald L. Sittser writes: "Grace has come to me in ways I did not expect. Friends have remained loyal and supportive in spite of my struggles."[5]

Remember too that the most trusted and loyal friend you have is Jesus Christ, "a man of sorrows and acquainted with grief" (Isaiah 53:3), who "will not fail you or forsake you" (Deuteronomy 31:6).

Don't Be Alarmed If You See Changes in Yourself

After the loss of a child, most parents perceive within themselves changes in their personal outlook on issues of life and death.[6] First, there is a sense that life has lost its innocence. Life has been shattered, like Humpty Dumpty, never to be put back together again. In addition, there can be an alteration in parents' perceptions of the control they exert over the lives of their children. In the past, before our child's death, it was comforting to suppose that we had some control over our children's safety and health. But now we know that however vigilant we may be, fate can intervene.

Mourning parents may also notice a profound change in our notion of values and priorities. One of the shifts in values is the aspiration to be more sensitive and compassionate in regard to the needs of others. Parents become more open to the tremendous amount of suffering in the world and acquire a new empathy for the anguish of others.

Also undergoing alteration is the value placed on work, money, acquisition, and status. The transience of life causes changes in the way our priorities are ordered, so it becomes more important for us to spend quality time with loved ones than to spend time acquiring the "things" of the world. For some, materialism and greed give way to love, compassion, and gaining the most from the present moment.

Inexplicably, when parents lose a child, they often find themselves gaining a new sense of empowerment. Bereaved parents have been through the most horrible ordeal a parent can suffer, and yet they have survived. Because they have lived through the death of a son or daughter, the worst life could present them has already happened. No matter what life gives them now, they can handle it. Harriet Sarnoff Schiff, author of *The Bereaved Parent*, aptly summarized the idea of empowerment: "The fear of the unknown is behind us, for most of us, because we have already taken a long look at hell."[7]

A child's death is a major change in life which causes many bereaved parents to re-evaluate their religious convictions. Various areas of doubts and questions are confronted in an attempt to clarify the meaning and the relevance of personal faith. Thus, the death of a child may provoke either a strengthening of faith or, conversely, a crisis of faith. Even parents who previously held strong religious convictions may find themselves struggling with religious concepts that do not seem to match up with the sorrows of life.

Somewhere in the course of the reevaluation, however, a doubting parent may catch a renewed glimpse of faith. He or she may see it in a golden sunrise, the softness of a baby chick, or the glory of a star-studded sky. Or, a parent may recognize it in acts of compassion and love bestowed during the course of bereavement. In that moment of truth, a parent may suddenly realize that something glorious and wonderful and pristine does indeed exists beyond this imperfect and painful and tarnished world in which we live.

Despite the fact that a parent doesn't have all the answers, and may never know all the "whys," he or she can cling once again with renewed hope and restored faith in a loving, gracious and compassionate God.

PREPARE YOURSELF TO DEAL
WITH HOLIDAYS AND ANNIVERSARIES

During holidays or anniversaries of important events, you will experience upsurges in grief. Some of these anniversary dates are more likely to remind you of your loved one. For instance, you may be especially saddened on the anniversary of your child's death or on his or her birthday. Other holidays such as Thanksgiving, religious celebrations, or Mother's or Father's Day are also times when you will be painfully reminded of your loss. Holidays are special occasions in our society when we are supposed to be together with our loved ones. For bereaved parents, these celebrations will be painful because your child can no longer participate in festivities.[8]

Since this will be a difficult time for your entire family, ask everyone, including other children, what they would like to do on holidays. Give your plans careful thought, and don't do anything that would put you or other family members in an emotional bind. It may be a good idea to trade in old memory-filled traditions and replace them with new comforting rituals. Or perhaps you might just want to alter your traditions slightly so that you don't have to highlight your loved one's absence more than it already is. For instance, you might want to have your Thanksgiving dinner or religious celebration at another relative's house instead of yours.

Keep in mind that plans for holidays can be changed from year to year. What you decide for this year can be changed next year if you want to go back to the old way. Just decide what is best for your family now and don't worry about holidays in years to come. You will be at a different place in your life in future years, so you can adapt at that time. The main concern is that you make the holidays more bearable for yourself while your grief is still fresh.

During this difficult time, consider doing something for someone else or reaching out to others, for this will bring you a measure of fulfillment and joy. When you're feeling deprived because of the loss of your child, perform an act of generosity, such as donating money to a needy cause in your loved one's name or volunteering to help out in a soup kitchen. By performing kindnesses such as this, you will be acting in the true spirit of the holidays and will not only be assisting others, but will also be helping yourself.

Blessed be the God ...of all comfort; who comforts us in all our afflictions so we may be able to comfort those who are in any affliction.

— 2 Corinthians 1:3-4

9

Engaging in Meaningful Activity

Although the length of the grieving process varies from parent to parent, you will eventually arrive at a bend in the road — at a gradual turning point where the seeds of renewed life will begin to take root. Relapses will recur, even when recovery is going well, because from time to time something will undoubtedly trigger a memory which brings grief flooding back in all its previous intensity. However, these bouts will become less frequent, last shorter periods of time, and become less intense.

The loss of a son or daughter requires a difficult and lengthy restructuring of identity because our identification with our children is so strong. It may take years for us to let go of that connection.[1] But when we let go, we are finally able to start taking pleasure in other interests and relationships.

Parents who seek and find meaningful pursuits and activities are better able to regain their sense of purpose and to revive their capacity for happiness. Renewing pleasure in your life will take courage because part of the grief of losing a child is feeling that your son or daughter was cheated of life's simple pleasures. Many parents think that giving up grief and permitting enjoyment is like stealing something that rightfully belonged to their child. To give up sadness not only feels disloyal, but also means relinquishing a vital link to their son or daughter.

Not so. It's okay to be happy. There is a time when you should again find yourself enjoying life and pursuing new interests. Although right now you may think you will never experience real joy again, that simply is not true. Happiness is a normal human emotion that is a vital part of God's will for your life, and, as time goes on, you will be able to more frequently experience that emotion.

BEGIN AN EXERCISE PROGRAM
WHEN YOUR HEALTH IMPROVES

When your physical health is improved and your emotional state is better, you might want to begin an exercise program. This will give you more energy and an improved outlook.

The exercise program you choose is up to you. The options include walking, jogging, lifting weights, cycling, or jumping rope. Body-work programs, such as polarity and reflexology or aerobic exercise, are excellent exercises you can also do on your own. You might also want to consider team sports, such as baseball, basketball, football, soccer, volleyball, and so forth.

Another alternative is to join a health club or spa where you could receive the benefits of access to a large variety of exercise equipment and a professional staff that can help in areas such as fitness, strength, cardio, or motivational training. Technical instruction can also be obtained through programs such as aerobic boxing, martial arts, and aerobic dance clubs. And conventional dance studios are great places to learn square dancing, tango, two-step, waltz, or the jitterbug.

Gardening and doing yard work are two other methods for getting physical exercise, as well as for planting seeds of hope in your psyche. Gardening can provide a calming, healing effect because it represents the beauty and growth of nature, as well as the natural cycles of life. You might want to plant a vegetable or flower garden outside or just begin with an indoor container or some indoor house plants.

Or try sprucing up your home. Splash on a coat of fresh paint on your living room, or choose a cheerful wallpaper. Rearrange the furniture, hang some new drapes, or place a fresh bouquet of flowers in a prominent place. These kinds of projects will leave you feeling better not only physically but emotionally as well.

VOLUNTEER YOUR TIME OR DONATE RESOURCES TO CHARITY

At some point, you may find yourself wanting to help others. If you are in early grief, you might want to postpone such activities, but, if you are in the later stages of grief, you might want to consider volunteering time to work at a mission, a homeless shelter, a nursing home, a Red Cross facility, or a service club.[2]

You might also be ready to reach out to help other mourners by volunteering at a hospice or by starting a support group. Many bereaved parents help out by organizing meetings, writing newsletters, and talking at length to the newly bereaved whenever they are needed.

Comforting other parents through support groups can be very rewarding, but one-on-one support is important, too. A phone call, a visit, a flower, a card, a hug or a word of encouragement are all important ways to connect to a parent who so desperately needs help.

The list of possibilities for things you can do is almost endless. What you do is not nearly as important as the fact that you are doing something, you are helping others.

If you don't have the time to volunteer, donating money or goods is another option. Make a charitable donation in your child's name. You will contribute to the welfare of others while also honoring your child's life. Scholarship funds or donations to charitable organizations such as Make-A-Wish Foundation (www.wish.org), Ronald McDonald's House (www.ronaldmcdonald.org), or St. Jude Children's Research Hospital (www.stjude.org) are excellent ways to donate in a child's name.

God's design for us is to bring ministry and comfort into the lives of others, as noted in 2 Corinthians 1:3-4: "Blessed be the God ... of all comfort; who comforts us in all our afflictions so that we may be able to comfort those who are in any affliction with the comfort with which we ourselves are comforted by God."

START AN ARTS AND CRAFTS PROJECT OR A NEW HOBBY

Crafts involve activities in which you make things with your own hands. One category of crafts involves textiles, such as cross-stitch, crocheting, dress-making, embroidery, knitting, lace-making, millinery, needlepoint, patchwork, quilting, rug-making, sewing, spinning, tapestry, tatting, and weaving.

Another category of crafts pertains to working with wood, metal, or clay. Metalworking, jewelry making, pottery, sculpture, and woodworking all fall under this category. Working with paper or canvas is another category which includes bookbinding, calligraphy, card-making, collage, decoupage, marbling, origami, paper-mache, parchment craft, quill work, scrap booking, and stamping.

You might want to create a memory book, which contains valued mementos of the child who died. You might consider including treasured photos, school work, newspaper clippings, hair clippings, and so forth. A memory book can help you heal. A memory quilt can be another way to commemorate a life that was lived. Phone others who knew and loved your son or daughter and ask them to contribute a quilt block.

Hobbies are also a good way for grieving parents to reconnect with life. Some of the more popular hobbies include stamp or coin collecting, scale model building, bird or butterfly watching, model railroading, genealogy, and cooking.

Reading is a hobby or activity that parents can pursue solely for entertainment or for the purpose of gaining knowledge in specific areas.

When your capacity for concentration returns and when you feel ready, head to your library or bookstore to get some books. There is nothing like a good book to divert your attention from the stresses of life. The options are many: mystery novels, science fiction, romance novels, historical nonfiction, gardening books, inspirational books, biographies, self-help books, cook books, or travel books.

Another source of helpful reading for mourning parents is study of Bible commentaries. At a time when we need to strengthen and improve our relationship with God, we can go deeper into the Word to obtain comfort, courage, and direction.

Traveling is another hobby. A short trip or an extended vacation can be both restorative and energizing. Sometimes a change of scenery can help us see our lives from a different perspective and can assist us in our search for meaning.

Writing can also be a very therapeutic hobby. The actual physical act of writing can be very rewarding intellectually and emotionally. And a collection of writings can help you reflect back on how you have progressed in your grief.

EXPLORE ARTISTIC PURSUITS

If you are interested in visual arts, you might enjoy drawing, painting, printmaking, sculpture, photography, pottery making or ceramics. Artistic expression through drawing or painting has been shown to be helpful for both adults and children as an outlet for releasing stressful feelings or pent-up emotions. So purchase some brushes, paints, and a canvas and paint your feelings about the death, or buy some charcoal and art paper to draw your emotions. In the process, don't be concerned about artistic abilities, but just let your imagination take charge.

Music also can be therapeutic, because it taps into the deep recesses of our emotions, both happy and sad. Most types of music can be healing.

You might even want to consider listening to a wide variety of music, perhaps even to sounds that aren't your normal fare.

If you sing or play an instrument, you might consider taking up music activities again. But if you don't have musical training, it's never too late to begin. Although some people can learn to perform or improvise music without special training, many feel the need for lessons.

The sub-titles of many Psalms indicate they were meant to be played on instruments or sung by a choir. For example, some state they were written for "stringed instruments," others for "flute [or other instrumental] accompaniment," while still others indicate they were written for the "choir director." Some simply add that they are "a song." No other book of hymns has been used for so long by so many people, earning it the title "The Hymnbook of the Ages." What a treasure!

GO BACK TO SCHOOL

The loss of a child has a way of making us rethink our priorities. Allow yourself the chance to restructure your life around the things that truly matter to you. For example, if you want to spend more time with family, but your job consumes too much time, ask your boss for a reduced working schedule, or if that isn't possible, look for another job. Alternatively, you might want to consider a new career and return to college or vocational school to train yourself for that career.

A study area you may find particularly rewarding is religious studies. If you feel a calling in regard to a specific area of ministry or even if you simply want to deepen your knowledge to personally minister to others, you will greatly benefit from a religious education.

JOIN A CLUB OR AN ORGANIZATION

You may find participation in social or service clubs or organizations enjoyable because they provide friendship, knowledge, skills, or service to others. Some examples of social clubs include: art clubs, book clubs, hobby clubs, game clubs, music clubs, motor clubs, political clubs, publishing clubs, religious clubs, social activities clubs, sports clubs, and yacht clubs. Familiar fraternal and service clubs or organizations are: Kiwanis, Lions Club, Rotary, Sierra Club, United Way, Veterans of Foreign Wars, and Volunteers of America.

Perhaps you might be interested in joining a Bible study club or in forming one yourself through your church. The main focus of a Bible club is spiritual growth through study of God's Word, sharing of feelings and thoughts, personal testimony, music, and prayer.

MEDITATE AND PRAY

In our intense suffering after the loss of a child, there can be times when we are too engrossed in grief to focus on faith. Only after we have faced our intense emotions are some of us able to refocus on our faith in God. On the other hand, during fresh grief, others of us may question our faith so that we will need to move forward more slowly.

But when you feel ready, it is important to get back in touch with your spirituality. Try to find a quiet time each day to meditate on God and to pray. Meditation is simply quiet contemplation in the presence of God. Particular techniques or rules do not exist. Just find a quiet place where you can think without distraction. Take a walk in the woods, sit beside a still stream, or just go to your bedroom and close the door.

Never underestimate the power of prayer. God makes it clear throughout His Word that when His children call Him, He hears. Pray for answers to your questions about life. Pray for God's healing touch and for the strength to bear your grief. Pray for other family members who are also in pain. If you have built a wall between yourself and God, pray that He will help you remove it. Keep in mind that God isn't forceful, but comes by invitation the moment you open your heart to Him. Move toward God, seek His face, and He will move toward you.

I came that they might have life, and might have it abundantly.

—John 10:10

10

Affirming Reality

Somewhere along the path of bereavement, the burden of your load will get lighter and the pain of your loss will lessen. The changes will go unnoticed at first because they are so subtle. At some point, however, you will arrive at the beginning of your recovery.[1]

You arrive at the point where your life starts to take on purpose and meaning again. Although this process will take a long time, you will experience changes in yourself that lead to a resolution of your grief. This will occur as you come to terms with your loss, form a new identity, strengthen family relationships, and restructure your life.

COME TO TERMS WITH YOUR LOSS

One of the characteristics of recovery involves coming to terms with your loss.[2] This happens when you have been able to process your grief to the point where you feel ready to move forward from the past. To do so, you will have to accustom yourself to the absence of your child in your life and adapt to the lack of interaction with the son or daughter who formerly contributed so much to your world.

Moving past your grief doesn't mean that you no longer think about or miss your deceased child, for that child is a part of your life forever. But his or her role in your life must necessarily change so you can move forward.[3] Although you must relinquish the role of loving your child as you did when he or she was physically present, you can replace that with the practice of loving your absent son or daughter through your memory of them. Memories of a deceased child are priceless and ageless.

Remember too, that your beloved child is in your future. Our understanding of our future home is often limited by our perspective. Often we think of heaven in a sort of abstract way as some far-off place that lacks substance or physical attributes. Yet our Lord spoke about heaven in terms that leave no doubt that our heavenly home is a real place: "In My Father's house are many dwelling places; if it were not so, I would have told you; for I go to prepare a place for you. And if I go and prepare a place for you, I will come again, and receive you to Myself; that where I am, there you may be also" (John 14:2-3).

FORM A NEW IDENTITY

After you come to terms with the reality of the loss of your child, you will need to form a new identity in order to rebuild your life. Recognize that the death of your child has changed you to a large degree and that you will never be the same person you were before he or she died. You will need to develop fresh beliefs and expectations about the world without your loved one. This task will be difficult because you will undoubtedly want the world to remain the way it was before your son or daughter died. You do not want to alter your feelings about the world and the way it works.

Nevertheless, you will need to give up certain hopes, dreams, expectations, and experiences you had with your child and develop new roles, skills, behaviors and relationships. By integrating your old and new selves together, you will be able to form a new identity.[4]

MOVE FORWARD IN FAMILY RELATIONSHIPS

The intense grief following a child's death can affect your remaining family relationships in either a positive or a negative manner.[5] For example, your relationships with remaining children can be permanently altered for better or for worse. Although parents will often recognize mistakes they made in dealing with surviving youngsters, and consequently note weaker family bonds, others will notice bonds that have grown stronger despite the blunders. Just as rivers change course after a torrential rain storm, relationships change course after the tempest of bereavement.

Likewise, marriage relationships can strengthen or collapse due to the tremendous strain placed upon the union by unmitigated grief. Some bereaved parents will notice a greater cohesiveness developing within the marriage as they are able to share their feelings, forgive each other, and rebuild their marriage into a stronger family unit. Unfortunately, others will be unable to mend the rift that has developed in the marriage friendship. Consequently, after the death of a son or daughter, some marriages will fail.

Although maintaining family relationships is important, it must be remembered that relationships cannot always be mended or restored despite our very best efforts. It can seem like an almost unbearable double whammy if you not only lose a child through death, but, then, also lose your spouse through divorce. At times, however, because misunderstandings can develop which seem insurmountable, the only option may be to accept imperfection within the marriage relationship with good grace and move forward.

Rejoice if your marriage stays intact, but accept reality if your relationship ends in divorce. Realize that you may need to eventually move past a broken marriage toward the possibility of a new healing and sustaining relationship. When the time is right for you to more actively reenter the social world, you may want to consider the possibility of dating again.[6] Church is a good place to meet new people. Dating services are also available and are a very efficient way to look for a partner.

Dating services generally require people to give personal information and to submit photographs in order to create profiles which include criteria such as age, race, gender, interests, religious affiliation, and so forth. Profiles are then posted so members can browse before deciding to communicate anonymously through the dating service. Members can engage in ongoing correspondence in order to get a sense of the personality, traits, and interests of another person. In this way, individuals can get to "know" one another and to better discern if someone meets their preferences in regard to both practical concerns and moral standards before meeting them.

A good dating service will provide detailed, specific instructions for your safety such as telling you to refrain from giving out personal information like your name, phone number, or address in your correspondence and advising you that your first meeting should be at a restaurant or other public place. Keep in mind that you will need to be cautious and careful because an individual can misrepresent him or herself by giving false information such as incorrect marital status, age, physical attributes or social/economic status. So be very careful. Nevertheless, the fact remains that many people have met their future spouses through dating services.

RESTRUCTURE YOUR LIFE

At some point, you will arrive at a place where you realize that you must make a decision in regard to your recovery. The loss of your son or daughter has left an indelible imprint on your soul, and you are a substantially different person. You need to know, however, that if you choose, you can return to happiness again. Life is full of risks. But if you fail to accommodate to the changes in your life, if you persist as if the world is still the same, then you will be failing to respond to the reality of your situation.[7]

You may be wondering what right you have to benefit from still being alive, since your child is dead. To answer that question, seriously consider what your child would want you to do. You have suffered an incredible loss and feel guilty about moving past the loss and attempting to reunite with life. What advice on this subject would your deceased child give you if he or she could? Really think about it. Your son or daughter would encourage you to move on, to refrain from dwelling on the past, but to face the future with courage and determination. Your child wouldn't want you to remain stuck with a permanent sense of sadness or inability to progress. Moving forward is the best tribute you can pay both to life itself and to the memory of your departed child who would want you to recover.

There are some steps you can take in moving forward toward a new life. Healthy grief resolution centers on such things as learning to live without your loved one, moving forward in the world despite your loss, and keeping those memories that are important to you alive in a special place of your heart. You will also need to understand your feelings, formulate new answers and priorities, and restructure your life in a meaningful way so you can go on living. By successfully dealing with the changes in your life, you will not only gain a better understanding of both yourself and others, you will also achieve a higher level of growth and positive development than you ever thought possible.

The choice is yours. From this moment on, make the choice to live your life to the fullest. For Jesus came that you "might have life, and might have it abundantly" (John 10:10).

*It is the blessing
of the Lord that
makes rich.*

— Proverbs 10:22

Final Comment

Although it has been over 32 years since Karen's death, seldom a day goes by that I do not think of her. Over the years, I have learned to say the words "I had a daughter who died" more calmly.

Bereaved parents are changed people. We are not the same as we were before our child's death. We are stronger and wiser, and we have more to give to others as we move past our own pain. Strength can arise out of our weakness, courage out of our fear, joy out of our sorrow, and new life out of our loss. Of course, there is also the possibility of a different outcome. There is danger that a grieving parent will become bitter and disillusioned about life, succumbing to fatalism and despair.

But those capable of facing loss in the knowledge that grief can be counted among the deepening experiences of life are able to count their blessings in spite of the pain. As Wolfelt explains, "You are blessed. Your life has purpose and meaning. This is not to deny the hurt, but it may help to consider the things that make your life worth living too. If you're feeling ready, make a list of the blessings in your life."[1]

For me, the list of blessings includes a deep realization of the worth of relationships, the benefits of love, the importance of lightheartedness, the significance of the present moment, and the value of faith. I hope that you, too, someday will be able to make your own list of blessings.

Norma Sawyers-Kurz

Web Site Resources

Compassionate Friends (International)
www.Compassionatefriends.org

The Bereaved Parents of the USA
www.bereavedparentsusa.org

The Candlelighters Childhood Cancer Fooundation
www.candlelighters.org

Mothers Against Drunk Driving (MADD)
www.madd.org

Parents of Murdered Children
www.pomc.com

Sudden Infant Death Syndrome Support
www.EarlyAngels.com

Pregnancy and Infant Loss Support
www.nationalshareoffice.com

Bibliography

Bernstein, Judith R. *When the Bough Breaks: Forever after the Death of a Son or Daughter.* Kansas City: Andrew McMeal Publishing, 1998.

D'Arcy, Paula. *Song for Sarah.* Wheaton, IL: Harold Shaw, 1979.

Hickman, Martha Whitmore. *I Will Not Leave You Desolate.* Nashville: The Upper Room, 1982.

Lewis, C. S. *A Grief Observed.* New York: The Seabury Press, 1961.

Manning, Doug. *Don't Take My Grief Away.* San Francisco: Harper & Row, 1984.

Mitsch, Raymond R. and Brookside, Lynn. *Grieving the Loss of Someone you Love.* Ann Arbor, MI: Servant Publications, 1993.

Noel, Brook. *Grief Steps: 10 Steps to Regroup, Rebuild, and Renew After any Life Loss.* Fredonia, WI: Champion Press, LTD., 2004.

O'Connor, Nancy. *Letting Go With Love: The Grieving Process.* Tucson, AZ: La Mariposa Press, 1984.

Rando, Therese A. *How to Go on Living When Someone You Love Dies.* New York: Bantam Books, 1991.

Salam, Harry and Cheryl. *From Grief to Glory: Rediscovering Life After Loss*. New Kensington, PA: Whitaker House, 2003.

Sanders, Catherine M. *How to Survive the Loss of a Child*. New York: Three Rivers Press, 1992.

Sanders, Catherine M. *Surviving Grief and Learning to Live Again*, New York: John Wiley and Sons, Inc., 1992.

Schiff, Hariet Sarnoff. *The Bereaved Parent*. New York: Penguin Books, 1977.

Sittser, Gerald L. *A Grace Disguised: How the Soul Grows Through Loss*. Grand Rapids: Zondervan Publishing House, 1995.

Vanauken, Sheldon. *A Severe Mercy*. New York: Harper Collins, 1977-1980.

Walsh, Chad. "Afterword," *A Grief Observed*. New York: The Seabury Press, 1976.

Westburg, Granger E. *Good Grief: A Constructive Approach to the Problem of Loss*. Minneapolis: Augsburg Fortress Press, 1997.

White, James R. *Grieving: Our Path Back to Peace*. Minneapolis: Bethany House Publishers, 1997.

Wolfelt, Alan D. *Healing Your Grieving Heart: 100 Practical Ideas*. Fort Collins, CO: Companion Press, 1998.

Notes

INTRODUCTION

[1]Paula D'Arcy, *Song for Sarah* (Wheaton, IL: Harold Shaw, 1979). As condensed from the book in *Reader's Digest*, December 1981, p. 220.

[2]See: Doug Manning, *Don't take My Grief Away* (San Francisco: Harper and Row, 1984); and Martha Whitmore Hickman, *I Will Not Leave You Desolate* (Nashville: The Upper Room, 1982).

[3]Excerpt from *A Severe Mercy* by Sheldon Vanauken (New York: HarperCollins Publishers, 1977, 1980.

[4]Chad Walsh, "Afterword," *A Grief Observed* (New York: The Seabury Press, 1976), p. 113.

CHAPTER 1

[1]See Granger E. Westberg, *Good Grief: A Constructive Approach to the Problem of Loss* (Minneapolis: Augsburg Fortress Press, 1979) for an excellent listing of the stages of grief.

[2]Catherine M. Sanders, *Surviving Grief and Learning to Live Again* (New York: John Wiley and Sons, Inc, 1992), p. 48.

[3]Therese A. Rando, *How to Go on Living When Someone You Love Dies* (New York: Bantam Books, 1991), p. 311.

[4]For additional information on support groups, including some Web sites, see the "Web Site Resources" at the end of this book.

[5]Alan D. Wolfelt, *Healing Your Grieving Heart: 100 Practical Ideas* (Fort Collins, CO: Companion Press, 1998), p. 67.

[6]Rando, p. 252.

[7]See Chapters 2 and 7 in this book for more details about health.

[8]Nancy O'Connor, *Letting Go With Love: The Grieving Process* (Tucson, AZ: La Mariposa Press, 1984), p. 19.

[9]Catherine M. Sanders, *How to Survive the Loss of a Child* (New York: Three Rivers Press, 1998), p. 17.

[10]Wolfelt, p. 4.

CHAPTER 2

[1]Granger E. Westberg, pp. 20-21.

[2]Rando, p. 248.

[3]James R. White, *Grieving: Our Path Back to Peace* (Minneapolis: Bethany House Publishers, 1997), p. 50.

[4]Westberg, p. 58.

[5]O'Connor, p. 153.

[6]C.S Lewis, *A Grief Observed* (New York: The Seabury Press, 1961), p. 53.

CHAPTER 3

[1]Judith R. Bernstein, *When the Bough Breaks: Forever After the Death of a Son or Daughter* (Kansas City: Andrews McMeal Publishing, 1998), p.30.

[2]See Bernstein, pp. 26-31, for more information about clinical depression.

[3]Sanders, *How to Survive the Loss of a Child*, pp. 10-11.

[4]Rando, p. 70.

[5]O'Connor, pp. 17-21.

[6]Ibid., pp. 159-161, 164.

[7]Bernstein, *When the Bough Breaks*, pp. 5-6.

[8]Sanders, *How to Survive the Loss of a Child*, p. viii.

[9]Ibid.

CHAPTER 4

[1]Rando, pp. 25-37

[2]Westberg, p. 43.

[3]Bernstein, pp. 80-81.

[4]Brook Noel, *Grief Steps: 10 Steps to Regroup, Rebuild, and Renew After Any Life Loss* (Fredonia, WI: Champion Press, 2004), pp.108-109.

[5]Sanders, *Surviving Grief and Learning to Live Again*, p. 126.

[6]Wolfelt, p. 57.

[7]Bernstein, p. 6.

CHAPTER 5

[1]O'Connor, p. 138-140.

[2]Rando, pp. 34-35.

[3]Sanders, *Surviving Grief and Learning to Live Again*, pp. 113-115.

[4]Ibid., p. 56.

CHAPTER 6

[1]Rando, p.29.

[2]Harry and Cheryl Salem, *From Grief to Glory: Rediscovering Life After Loss* (New Kinsington, PA: Whitaker house, 2003), p. 95.

[3]See Sanders, *How to Survive the Loss of a Child*, p. 58, for more information about displaced anger.

[4]O'Connor, pp. 34-35.

[5]Sanders, *How to Survive the Loss of a Child*, p.59.

[4]Noel, p. 129.

CHAPTER 7

[1]Sanders, *Surviving Grief and Learning to Live Again*, pp. 80-81.

[2]O'Connor, p. 166.

[3]Sanders, *Surviving Grief and Learning to Live Again*, pp. 102-103.

[4]O'Connor, pp. 135, 170-179.

[5]Salem, p. 64.

[6]This quote is taken from a Web MD archive feature, "Is Religion Good Medicine?" by Salynn Boyles (March 13, 2002), which discusses both sides of the debate over the link between religion and health.

CHAPTER 8

[1]Rando, pp. 171-173.

[2]Sanders, *How to Survive the Loss of a Child*, pp. viii, 10.

[3]See Sanders, *Surviving Grief and Learning to Live Again*, p. 175, for more on children's bereavement.

[4]Noel, pp. 201-204.

[5]Gerald L. Sittser, *A Grace Disguised: How the Soul Grows Through Loss* (Grand Rapids: Zondervan Publishing House, 1995), p. 114.

[6]Bernstein, pp. xv, 70-81.

[7]Harriet Sarnoff Schiff, *The Bereaved Parent* (New York: Penguin Books, 1981), p. 144.

[8]Wolfelt, pp. 40-42.

CHAPTER 9

[1]Sanders, *How to Survive the Loss of a Child*, p. 37.

[2]See Bernstein, pp. 75-76, 214-219, for more information on ways to volunteer time or donate resources.

CHAPTER 10

[1]Sanders, *How to Survive the Loss of a Child*, p. 36.

[2]O'Connor, p. 27.

[3]Bernstein, pp. 15-25.

[4]Sanders, *Surviving Grief and Learning to Live Again*, p. 91.

[5]O'Connor, p. vii.

[6]Rando, pp. 297-299.

[7]Ibid., pp. 16-19.

FINAL COMMENT

[1]Wolfelt, p. 96.

Index

A

affirming reality, 5, 25,101
anger, 5, 25, 35, 44, 45, 49, 62, 66, 69-75, 79, 86
anniversaries, 57, 85, 90
ashamed, 28, 36, 43, 50, 69

B

Bereaved Parents of the USA, 48, 109
Bernstein, Judith R., 43, 44, 48, 54, 58, 89, 96, 101, 103, 111
blame, 61, 63, 64, 70, 72
blessings, 107
Boyles Salynn, 66
Brookside, Lynn, 119

C

Candlelighters Childhood Cancer Foundation, 109
charity, 95
children, 7, 15, 28, 63, 65, 71, 85-89, 91, 93, 102, 109
communicate, 63, 71, 86, 104
Compassionate Friends, 48, 109
conservation, 47

H

I-K

L

M

N-O

P

R

S

Start a Support Group!

The Grieving Parent's Book of Hope makes an ideal 12-week support group text. Hold a get-started session, then meet once a week for 10 weeks and discuss one of the chapters each meeting. Have a final meeting based on the Final Comments section. To contact Norma about speaking engagements, email her at normasawyerskurz@aol.com.